GOOD IS NOT GOOD ENOUGH

TO ASSIST YOUR ORGANIZATION TO UNLOCK IT'S POTENTIAL IN CULTURE BY INCREASING EMPLOYEE HAPPINESS, INNOVATION, AND PRODUCTIVITY.

DR. AMIT DAS

To

All my bosses who made a difference in my professional career.

"Excellence

Is a narrow singularity of greatness.

Difficult to stand on, and

Even more difficult to stay on,

Excellence moves.

We are either

Moving toward excellence

Or moving away from it.

Excellence does not stand still.

Excellence pushes the limits

Of positivity and possibility.

Excellence can only be reached

After it has long been pursued and almost achieved.

Excellence is interwoven

With human frailty, failure, and experience,

Making it ten-fold stronger fabric than average.

Excellence does not break when flexed.

Achieving excellence

Gives one unique insight

Into the future and the possibilities,

Paving the way

To even greater bursts of excellence."

-By Leo Thomas

Contents

Foreword *vii*

Preface *xiii*

Acknowledgements *xvii*

1. Introduction 1

2. Business Transformation 15

3. Sustainable Excellence 27

4. Value Reorientation 37

5. Developing Culture 55

6. Critical Communication 76

7. Competitive Advantages 87

8. Leadership Capabilities 107

9. Trusting Environment 119

Conclusions 145

Suggestions 149

About The Author 161

References 163

Foreword

"When everything seems to be going against you, remember that the airplane takes off against the wind, not with it." - Henry Ford

The level of competition is rising. Internal dysfunctions hinder the ability to address important issues. There are no clearly defined strategies. Organizational procedures and structures aren't set up to supply the strategies that are required. Employees aren't aligned, motivated, or capable of delivering at a high level, and corporate cultures don't encourage competitive differentiation practises. The first and most important step to increasing morale is to focus on supporting and resourcing your staff. Remember, if you make the effort to create a great corporate culture, your firm will prosper. A healthy culture is a typical feature of strong companies. Your corporate culture is simply the way you operate together, the sum of your team's values and practises. The issue is that, whether you're paying attention or not. So, how can you nurture the culture you desire? Dr. Amit Das provides a step-by-step approach in this book on how to create an excellent culture at your firm. The author demonstrates how to uncover your hidden culture, set up feedback loops, transform ideals into actions, and open up communication across layers. To keep your culture thriving for the long term, the author emphasizes the significance of being clear from the top, building trust, and providing support structures. As Dr. Amit Das demonstrates in his book, by building your culture, you can increase communication, raise morale, encourage trust, and keep negativity at bay within your team.

You will learn how to uncover your current cultural system, identify your target, brilliant culture, design solutions with participation from all organizational levels, develop action plans to instil new mindsets, behaviours, and structures, and make listening, trust, and truth-telling an essential part of your organization by reading this book. The author provides businesses with a step-by-step strategy for analysing, creating, and implementing iterative cultural transformation, with each success building on prior achievements. As a result, the company continues to adapt in ways that reduce stress, encourage learning, and promote organizational wellness.

"To achieve excellence in anything, first knowledge is the need;
A vision based on whole knowledge helps to fix a broad ambition
That always helps as driving force to move ahead in one's venture;
With experience and ideas one makes strides by intelligent moves!"

It's difficult to comprehend the extent to which creativity has influenced your life. Imagine being able to snap your fingers and make all the results of human creativity—everything man-made—disappear. What would happen if your world changed? The creative process results in reality. Reality is constructed by humans. Understanding how the creative process becomes stifled and understanding how to release its force and energy turns creativity into execution excellence. Excellence refers to how well a strategy is carried out.

Countless business professionals strive to be successful leaders. The actual aim for industrious, growth-oriented top performers who are never content with the status quo and rigorous thinkers who are never satisfied with the status quo is the lifetime pursuit of perfection. Dr. Amit Das has interviewed hundreds of the most prolific performers to learn the best strategies for pursuing and maintaining organizational greatness. He discovered a pattern of unusual actions that distinguished these exceptional people. You'll learn how to: commit to yourself and the process-and develop purpose, focus, and discipline; develop resilience to face new challenges and find inspiration for the long haul; seek guidance-and lead others to new heights; meet the moment-and make the most of every opportunity to excel; and build a trusted group of advisors-and become a lifelong learner by following his examples. With the pursuit of excellence, you can put your attitudes into action and convert your actions into habits. You refer to this human yearning for greater and better things as the pursuit of human perfection. You all have the necessary tools to achieve greatness. They are, however, mainly inactive. You must make concerted efforts to reach your full potential. The book *"Good Is Not Good Enough"* delves into how and where these efforts must be made in order for this to happen. The book is the result of the author's own endeavour to improve organizational performance. The most current concepts, as well as new observations and opinions, have been chosen and assembled. It will be extremely beneficial to the readers in their pursuit of perfection.

The author offers the most effective tactics and step-by-step instructions for you to construct your own particular road to excellence in this book. You'll learn how to concentrate on achieving greatness while living and enjoying life to the fullest. You'll develop a more optimistic attitude, more concentrated dedication, better ways to deal with distractions and demands, and tactics for conquering challenges. You'll also find better methods to collaborate with colleagues, respond more effectively to coaching and mentoring, and become more positive and self-directed in your thoughts and actions, resulting in more personal and professional pleasure.

This book attempts to provide insights into the many pathways, courses, and drives that world-class enterprises have constructed in order to achieve the pinnacles of greatness. It also includes an empirical analysis of leadership, a simple and practical conceptual model of what leadership is, and an actionable guide for developing competitive spirit, achieving sustained performance, achieving durable influencing capacity, assisting others in bringing change, and assisting in the actualization of human potential in all roles and levels. It contains the ideas, views, experiences, beliefs, viewpoints, and forward-thinking thoughts of some of the best management and business minds in the world.

Organizations do not adapt quickly enough to keep up with changing requirements, and governance and management methods do not generate the required results. Ineffective communication exacerbates these issues. The development of a good Organization Performance System can help to solve these issues. The contents of this book will provide a deep reservoir of ideas and techniques for producing remarkable outcomes, competitive advantage, and long-term results for leaders, consultants, and organization advisors. The book *"Good Is Not Good Enough"* draws on firsthand experience from high-performance operations to deliver vital leadership lessons as well as clear, accessible, and practical insights on managing teams in any corporate setting.This book provides a new and fascinating viewpoint on the factors that influence team and organizational greatness. Dr. Amit Das, the book's author, has a unique combination of expertise and insight, having worked as a management consultant. His insights and interviews from business sectors are used to demonstrate the obstacles to high performance and leadership.

The materials include a performance model that can be applied to a wide range of organizations, focusing on people attitude rather than skills; a process for closing the gap between desired and actual outcomes; how to accelerate performance in real time; exhibiting a set of behaviours that others choose to follow; and avoiding the victory of compliance over outcomes. The author reconstructs the determinants of high performance with uncommon clarity, insight, and accessibility in this book, illustrating and explaining concrete tools and strategies that readers may use in their own teams and organizations.

This book discusses how businesses may cope with human fallibility in order to foster workplace excellence. Some workplace blunders endanger lives, while others pave the way for inventive innovations. An company requires a communication atmosphere where it is acceptable to express viewpoints, confess mistakes, and seek for support in crucial situations in order to cope constructively with fallibility.

This book focuses on emotional intelligence, which has been identified as a factor in excellent on-the-job performance and the capacity to live a successful life. The book deviates from typical methodologies by emphasizing on non-cognitive rather than cognitive skills to explain and predict performance and achievements. It is based on a rising country, India. It finds that those with strong intrinsic non-cognitive skills such as trustworthiness, conscientiousness, adaptability, initiative, and commitment have a better chance of becoming effective leaders with enhanced service-orientation, empathy, and conflict management skills—all of which are desirable traits in any organization striving for efficiency. It also indicates that, while such intangible, internal talents are important, they cannot replace obvious psycho-social characteristics and that, as a result, effective recruiting tactics must include behavioural as well as cognitive skills.

The world has changed. The previous method of managing (but not resolving) employee conflict is no longer effective. Every organization's openness has risen as a result of social media, and our shifting demographics make it more crucial than ever to be genuine and foster a healthy working culture. The # MeToo movement is the result of employers' resolving conflicts in the wrong way. That doesn't imply, as you'll see in *"Good Isn't Good Enough,"* taking steps that might put you at risk of claims. It entails broadening your perspective and treating the workplace as a whole, rather than just focusing on the symptoms (claims) of a toxic workplace culture. You'll learn about the core causes of workplace critical situation, as well as what is most likely to lead to sexual harassment at work, which is very pertinent in today's context. Given that we are in the midst of a cultural shift over what constitutes suitable and incorrect workplace behavior, the themes discussed in this book are a must-read for any company leader, rising leader, or employee who wants to understand how to avoid any workplace critical situation.

The capacity of an organization to function efficiently, adapt properly, adjust correctly, and grow from within is referred to as organizational health. People, processes, structures, systems, behaviours, and governance are all characteristics of a good company. It's one in which suitable adaptation, maintenance, and development actions are critical to preserving operational performance and alignment. Organizational health examines the key and interrelated parts of an organization that must be kept in good working order for managers to achieve their objectives. Understanding and assessing organizational health; the impact of structures on organizational health, such as hierarchies, alliances, and joint ventures; maintenance and development, including organizational development, change management, learning, and workplace environment; sustainability, including carbon footprint and business ecosystems; and indicators of health and dysfunction are all covered using a practical, structured approach.

Prepare for limited performance and poor outcomes if you're locked in an old leadership paradigm. With the pace of change increasing by the day, it's more critical than ever to cultivate a positive and enabling culture. In this business manual on leadership excellence, you will learn to excite and engage people; fix problems that will have an immediate impact on your bottom line; distinguish between management and leadership; and assist employees overcome their toughest hurdles. The author also looks at whether great leaders are born or made, how lean ideas are used differently in various organizations, and why clever individuals fail so often after being promoted to management positions. Take a path that leads to significant performance increases and a great culture where everyone is prepared to succeed with this leadership.

Preface

"The achievements of an organization are the results of the combined effort of each individual." – Vince Lombardi

This book presents a research-based, actionable methodology and metric for measuring organizational excellence to assist managers in creating productive and results-oriented workplaces. It explains why the top organizations in the world, such as Starbucks, Southwest Airlines, Amazon, Google, and Apple, thrive in leadership. Organizational excellence is a thought-provoking and emotionally rewarding philosophy of organizational transformation that has relevance and application in the workplace.

This book is also about you—there are so many different aspects of your existence in the complicated world you live in: internal, external, and personal life; family life, job life, professional life, and social life. Each aspect of life has its own set of challenges and worries. You are not a single homogeneous bunch, either. You belong to a variety of organizations and have a variety of identities, including economic, political, social, religious, cultural, national, racial, and so on. Despite all of your differences and similarities, there are many things that you all share in common. Above all, you are all human beings. Human senses and sensibilities are identical within you. Everyone has the ability to feel, think, experience, and reflect. You all want to live in a more comfortable and delightful environment, and you all want to improve, progress, and improve your life.The final aim remains the same, whether you're an aspiring leader or an entrepreneur: to realise your full potential, you all want to improve, progress, and improve your lives.

"

"A mind full of ideas only can think of achieving excellence
In any field one aspires to do remarkable thing in the world;
Dreams only generate ideas to such an active mind of a person
To realize all dreams one day or other in the world of chances!"

The author offers the most effective tactics and step-by-step instructions for you to construct your own particular road to excellence in this book. You'll learn how to concentrate on achieving greatness while living and enjoying life to the fullest. You'll develop a more optimistic attitude, more concentrated dedication, better ways to deal with distractions and demands, and tactics for conquering challenges. You'll also find better methods to collaborate with colleagues, respond more effectively to coaching and mentoring, and become more positive and self-directed in your thoughts and actions, resulting in more personal and professional pleasure. Although particular criteria may change over time, few goals in education are considered more essential than achieving professional competence.

Today, business psychologists and other social scientists have a variety of perspectives on this topic. One evident flaw in the argument is the division between those who prioritise individual development and those who focus on cultural and organizational transformation. Author gives a variety of ideas on how to foster organizational excellence in this book. This allows individuals who prioritize organizational practise reform and those who highlight individual skills to communicate with one another, and invites readers to explore the reasons for both perspectives, or a hybrid of the two. The aim is to think about how these two opposing perspectives might be harmonised, or at the very least coordinated, to benefit both individuals and organizations as a whole. The central argument is that quality may be cultivated without jeopardising equity, which are both important elements of a democratic organization.

The problems raised in this book have ramifications and importance in the domains of organizational psychology, practises and culture, organizational excellence philosophy, and organizational leadership. The book also examines organizations' aim to create a dynamic and happy working atmosphere in order to avoid unproductive or disruptive forces and ensure increased performance over time. Corporate employees, as well as scholars and practitioners of the subject, will find the book useful. *"Good Is Not Good Enough"* lays out a structure for managers or leaders to follow in order to increase company performance in all sorts of businesses.

Acknowledgements

At the outset I will thank to my family for supporting me throughout the journey of writing my book and encouraging me to live my dreams- my son has always been instrumental in giving his inspiration to complete the writing of this book. Despite the fact that I am listed as the author of this book, "Good is Not Good Enough" would not have been published if I had depended entirely on my own talents. To create this book required more than anything —it took a family of dedicated and caring people who were always prepared to lend a hand.

Writing a book while working full-time is no simple task, so I'd want to express my gratitude to my amazing coworkers, who act as mentors and cheerleaders in equal measure. Thank you, too, to the rest of the accumentor team for your patience and unflinching support while I worked on this book!

Thank you to everyone who has listened to me argue for doing everything you can to make your life, including your work life, more progressive. I appreciate everyone's assistance throughout the process. This book would not have been possible without each of you having had an impact on my life in some manner.

I would like to thank all the people whom I have been associated, you gave me power. I would like to thank Notion Press for publishing my book. At last thank you all for gifting your time to read out this book.

Lastly, I'd want to convey my heartfelt appreciation to the Almighty God for bestowing his blessings and being so gracious.

CHAPTER ONE

INTRODUCTION

A Deeper Understanding Of The Key Drivers Of Organizational Excellence

"Desire is the key to motivation, but it's determination and commitment to the unrelenting pursuit of your goal-a commitment to excellence-that will enable you to attain the success you seek."

-Mario Andretti

As I sat down at my computer today to write a book about transforming mediocrity into greatness and bringing out the best in people, I realized how much mediocrity envelops this nation, the ostensibly last frontier. Some of you are like fireflies in this darkness, with the will and capacity to shine small lights of greatness in your little corners. Excellence is not about being the greatest in the world; it is about being the best you can be and always pushing the boundaries. Whether it's boiling a cup of coffee, baking a loaf of bread, constructing a website, or developing a company development plan, how you do it reveals who you are to others around you. There is a significant difference between pushing the limits and doing what is adequate. So, wherever you are, the first step in building an atmosphere for greatness is to light up others by being an inspiration to them.

Instill in everyone around you the notion that being good enough is an embarrassment. The aim here is not to reach the KPIs or sales targets, but to smash them and set some records along the way. You strive for client joy rather than consumer contentment. You test the boundaries not because someone tells you to, but because it's who you are. Most importantly, this practice of pushing the limits for greatness is not a fad or a passing fad that fades after certain milestones for each of you, but rather a lifelong habit that pervades and governs all activities of your lives.

The first step in leading by example is to set a good example. As a result, you must establish pushing the boundaries as an organizational priority and design a mechanism that regularly acknowledges and promotes individuals who do so. To accomplish so, you must have complete clarity on the vision we are attempting to attain, as well as all actionable targets along the way, since ambiguity fosters mediocrity. The burden of removing uncertainty in the workplace lies on the shoulders of team leaders, and this is likely where the majority of the work is. This lets you relate your workplace to going to the gym. First, you must motivate individuals to desire to be stronger. Second, instil in the community the importance of always pushing the boundaries. Third, provide quantification tools and clear actionable targets so that everyone understands where they stand today and how far they still need to go.

Healthy cultures may be found in all outstanding organizations. Simply said, your corporate culture is the way you work together. For better or worse, the total of your team's values and actions will colour it. Great organizations are built on a strong culture. So, by enhancing culture, you will increase communication, raise morale, and encourage trust. If your organization is like others, you've witnessed culture emerge organically. It's probable that you haven't spent the necessary time building it, and culture will flourish with or without your attention. Cultivating the desired culture is a bit more challenging. You are a company that serves around 500,000 people every year and has nearly 2,000 employees. It's a major thing to figure out how to work together, how to be a team, and how to respect one another. Companies are eager to find methods to distinguish themselves, to position themselves as desirable employers, and to promote themselves as organizations deserving of victory in the battle for talent. Calls for a vibrant workplace culture to be the secret weapon in making all of this a reality abound. In corporate the term *"workplace culture"* has become commonplace. Despite all of the hype about how important culture is, few firms truly put in the effort to create and maintain a healthy and productive work environment. Although research shows that a healthy culture improves company performance, little emphasis is devoted to how to build and maintain a healthy culture.

This book will give you a plan to recognize, prevent, and resolve workplace challenges, whether your business is already on its way to the top of the healthy workplace culture pyramid or you're beginning from scratch. And whether you're a leader, an aspiring leader, or an employee looking to avoid unnecessary drama, the advice in this book will help you contribute to the answer we're all looking for: a workplace free of it. It's important to remember that a healthy culture is also a pleasant culture. It is a common myth that in order to be conflict-free, you must eliminate all forms of entertainment and amusement. But who wants to work in a place like that? A healthy, inclusive, and respectful culture should also be fun.

The roots of a negative work culture acknowledging the core reasons for drama is just as crucial as identifying and recognizing it (ideally early, when it may still be readily handled). Any one of these scenarios, let alone a combination of them, has the ability to destroy your business. Genuine leadership The idea that management is hypocritical, that they merely speak the talk but don't walk the walk, is created or perpetuated by a lack of authenticity. Employees lose enthusiasm for their employment, passion for what the firm represents, and, most dangerously, trust in this climate.

This book will give you a plan to recognize, prevent, and resolve workplace challenges, whether your business is already on its way to the top of the healthy workplace culture pyramid or you're beginning from scratch. And whether you're a leader, an aspiring leader, or an employee looking to avoid unnecessary drama, the advice in this book will help you contribute to the answer we're all looking for: a workplace free of it. It's important to remember that a healthy culture is also a pleasant culture. It is a common myth that in order to be drama-free, you must eliminate all forms of entertainment and amusement. But who wants to work in a place like that? A healthy, inclusive, and respectful culture should also be fun.

The roots of a negative work culture acknowledging the core reasons for drama is just as crucial as identifying and recognizing it (ideally early, when it may still be readily handled). Any one of these scenarios, let alone a combination of them, has the ability to destroy your business. Genuine leadership The idea that management is hypocritical, that they merely speak the talk but don't walk the walk, is created or perpetuated by a lack of authenticity. Employees lose enthusiasm for their employment, passion for what the firm represents, and, most dangerously, trust in this climate.

In a nutshell, workplace culture refers to your company's beliefs, values, and habits. Employee engagement, employee satisfaction, happiness at work, compensation, benefits, and other workplace perks are just a few of the factors that define and assess the health of a workplace culture. Individual aspects are often confused with defining a culture. There are several components to a good and thriving workplace culture. You can't ascend to the highest rungs of Maslow's hierarchy of requirements without first addressing fundamental needs.

The author of this book wants to provide you with a step-by-step guide to assist you in creating an excellent culture at your firm. The author will discuss how to get your team on a mission together. He'll teach you how to communicate clearly from the top, create trust, and set up some support structures to keep your culture flourishing. Finally, the author will provide you with some hands-on ways to nourish your culture over time. So, if you're ready to make a change or transform your organization.Your cultural ethos informs your sense of social purpose. What about your cultural ethos, though? And knowing what you're truly about, your cultural ethos, will not only help you hire the appropriate people, but it will also help you keep them on goal together. So, how do you persuade people to work together on a mission? It's a lengthy road, but the author offers a few pointers to get you started. Organizational culture has piqued scholars' interest, with a particular focus on the relationship between culture and organizational performance. However, the link between organizational culture and commercial success, as well as how to attain exceptional performance, remains a mystery. A mediocre culture exists in a company that provides the essentials—a fair salary and benefits package, as well as a generally safe working environment.People come to work to earn a living. Profits are stagnant, and there is little innovation. Companies that fail to offer even these fundamental services have toxic cultures, and this toxicity eventually kills the company's potential to prosper. A good culture is one in which a firm goes above and beyond by providing additional benefits and taking measures to ensure that its employees are engaged and connected. Their personnel are aware of the company's objective and feel connected to it as well as to one another. In terms of employee relations, these businesses concentrate on and adhere to the law.

Then there are the businesses with wonderful work environments. The success of these businesses may be attributed to three factors: Because culture refers to the conventions that govern how people approach issues and generate solutions, these organizations regard preventing, managing, and overcoming conflict as an important component of their culture. And the outcomes are undeniable: a cohesive and collaborative workplace that fosters creativity and, as study after study has demonstrated, improves sales and profits

"Good Is Not Good Enough" is a new research and opportunity reference that looks at the link between corporate culture and commercial performance. This book is appropriate for business professionals, managers, researchers, and academicians, and it

highlights subjects such as cultural excellence and individual productivity. When there is an organizational culture that aligns and motivates people; an effective strategy that delivers value in response to client priorities; processes and systems that produce efficient, high-quality work; an organizational structure that empowers people and facilitates workflow; and a strategy that recruits, develops, and retains the right people, the best results are produced. The correct balance between the total and the parts is found in a great organization. As a result, in order to be exceptional for a long time, an organization must master the art of change management. This book is meant to give the necessary tools for attaining a deeper understanding of the key drivers of organizational excellence.

Recent business trends have caused firms to undertake transformations at a faster rate than ever before, and as a result, the importance of human resources has grown. Though there has been extensive research in the field, with the changing paradigm, an attempt has been made through this book to determine the current state of organizations and examine the impact of an emerging aspect of the transformative cultural context on achieving organizational excellence in both the Indian and global contexts.

Excellence is the result of continually achieving your best in all that you do. Excellence is regularly performing ordinary things extremely well. Create awareness, create excellence, and follow through with excellence in execution goes above and beyond anything else on the market in terms of equipping leaders with the tools they need to become exceptional in execution.This practical guide will assist you in precisely assessing your company's present situation and developing a plan that will optimize its future success. Dr. Amit Das expands on themes provided in his books, The power of understanding people and the power of understanding, by offering fresh applications, practical real-world techniques, and strong organizational evaluation tools, among other things.

Leadership alignment, leadership philosophy, corporate culture, employee experience, and customer experience are among the important aspects of organizational success discussed in the book. Each thorough chapter explains a fundamental component of peak performance culture, including a clear explanation, examples, expert insights, and practical considerations applicable to a variety of real-world scenarios. Whether your firm is struggling with performance issues or is currently successful but aspires to even greater heights, a peak performance culture can help.

Leaders now realize that they must be able to design strategy as well as execute it. However, practically all books, blogs, presentations, articles, and other materials focus on *"why"* execution is vital rather than *"how"* to execute well. Excellence in execution seeks to pick up where the majority of others drop off. It focuses on transforming leaders' present mindsets and attitudes. It is divided into two parts and takes the reader on a journey of implementation. Two-thirds of strategy of executions still fail, necessitating a new method. Strategy Cadence, execution juxtaposition, and deciphering the execution problem are some of the new words offered. It focuses on transforming leaders' present mindsets and attitudes. Two-thirds of strategy executions still fail, necessitating a new method. Strategy Cadence, execution juxtaposition, and deciphering the execution problem are some of the new words offered. Create awareness, create excellence, and follow through with excellence in execution. This goes above and beyond anything else on the market in terms of equipping leaders with the tools they need to become exceptional in execution. Prepare for limited performance and poor outcomes if you're locked in an old leadership paradigm. With the pace of change increasing by the day, it's more critical than ever to cultivate a positive and enabling culture. In this business manual to leadership excellence, Author explores how to: excite and engage people; address problems that have a direct impact on your bottom line; distinguish between management and leadership; and assist employees in overcoming their toughest hurdles. The author also looks at whether great leaders are born or made, how lean ideas are used differently in various organizations, and why clever individuals fail so often after being promoted to management positions.

Employees appear to be more desirous of meaningful, purpose-driven employment than at any other moment in history. Big companies and social entrepreneurship have grown in popularity over the past decade. It's all over the news. Non-profits are no longer the only ones whose activities should result in some social good. Employees want more from their employers than vague promises about community involvement and social responsibility.They seek businesses with a social mission, businesses that combine social benefit with commercial ambitions. Employees now have a clear mandate.

Organizational excellence, according to the book, is a well-defined destination. Companies may structure their operations in such a way that they achieve and sustain excellence.With this system, any employee can detect any problem as soon as it arises and rectify it as quickly as possible so that activities may continue uninterrupted. The book lays out a step-by-step process for creating an ideal organization, making organizational excellence simple to accomplish.

What social good motivates your team to work together on a mission? If you don't know, you should find out. And when you do, you must raise it and document it. Talk about it, and make it something your team rallies behind when things get difficult, tense, or expensive. Now the flag isn't just for show; you'll need to carry it to the battlefield. In his executive coaching practise, the author has worked with several businesses that have a rallying cry that serves as their banner. So, how are you assisting your people in finding a match under your banner? These shared experiences will aid in the strengthening of ties in your cultural ethos. They foster enthusiasm and ensure buy-in. To truly cement this cultural attitude, your team must discuss it. So, you want to make it possible for your people to share their combat memories and celebrate victories together. Schedule time for teams to communicate about their common work, celebrate triumphs together, and support one another in their jobs. And, more importantly, to remind each other why their job is important. Soon, you'll see that some of these victories will become business folklore, shared memories that capture your culture. Hearing about these experiences will inspire new team members to make their own memories. So, do you have a logo? Is your team aware of it? If not, make it so.

The book covers the numerous characteristics of organizational leadership and the implications they have on important outcomes such as employee behaviours, work satisfaction, team creativity and innovation, and organizational success, based on multiple rigorous research studies in Western and Eastern cultures. The book presents a measurement instrument that may be used for organizational culture evaluation, selection, and training, as well as developing strategies to exploit organizational leadership's behavioural aspects at the personal, team, and organizational levels.

This multifold issue, according to the author, necessitates the development of an organizational excellence programme that fits and flourishes in these multicultural cultures. In response, he examines corporate practises in business excellence frameworks that have been widely employed to promote organizational performance on a global scale. Effective leadership practises are addressed in the book as a component that is no longer an option, but rather a need for firms to succeed in more globalised markets.

Organizational energy is a strong and tried-and-true strategy for transforming businesses. Its strength arises from a new view of organizations as living systems with their own vital energy, rather than as mechanical machines chasing financial goals. Leaders may understand and develop business excellence from a new viewpoint and improve the health and profitability of their businesses by using the analogy between the human energy system and the organizational energy system. This new mindset represents a fundamental change in business toward more sustainable ways of engaging people and managing our finite resources. Author offers such a path in this book, by going beyond the traditional, restricted mechanical models of organizations and toward a more fluid and holistic view of organizations and their surroundings. According to the author, you must enhance your organizational consciousness. Also, you must learn to behave with a deeper grasp of the current corporate landscape's interconnectedness.

The importance of strategic direction is explained in this book. Understanding your company's purpose, its applied metrics, strategic communications, strategic hiring, purposeful culture, relational trust, employee empowerment, and work environment optimization are all important steps in achieving organizational excellence. This book assesses the prevalent winning culture in selected organizations based in India and across the globe, covering all major business sectors.

The book will be useful to business leaders since it tries to suggest some practical solutions for firms to improve their current processes. All big firms have information technology woven into their fabric. From enhancement to assurance of effectiveness, it has evolved into a guiding factor for corporate excellence. Organizational excellence is a long-term competitive advantage that allows a company to outlast its competitors. Organizations that have remained good for a long time have some characteristics, such as allocating more resources and attention to particular crucial areas. The topic of key drivers of organizational excellence is timely in the intensely competitive business climate that every company in every industry faces. Many businesses are obsessed with metrics, but often neglect to focus on and control performance drivers. It's crucial to understand the difference. Performance is produced by key drivers, and performance is measured by keyindicators.The most important factor is the alignment of the five drivers: organizational culture, strategy, processes, structure, and people.

Organizations nowadays use a variety of techniques to entice customers and retain the brand's image for a long time. Manufacturers can't always rely on off-the-shelf equipment to meet their manufacturing needs. Organizations are strengthening and competenting their supply chains in order to be more effective and efficient. As the cliché goes, the toughest task is to recognise each and every person as an individual with distinct selling propositions. Leadership and management overlap are important, especially when a lot is expected to be accomplished in a short amount of time.

This work enumerates all of the practical subtleties of process implementation, as well as the modest yet successful procedures made to match the company's business and strategic objectives. There has been an effort to evolve and guarantee that a generic approach is used. There is reason to assume that the majority of the procedures and recommendations discussed above can be applied to practically all businesses. It examines both innovation and entrepreneurship, as well as why they matter in an increasingly competitive and turbulent world, and recommends strategies for firms to develop their entrepreneurial ability using accessible approaches and initiatives.

Organizational creativity is a powerful competitive advantage in every company, yet it is frequently undervalued. The first step in becoming an innovative company is to encourage people to be creative. The concept of radiant and visual thinking via mind maps is readily helpful in generating new ideas or conquering difficulties in an organization. The secret to building a successful company is to scale up excellence. It's how a small business grows without losing its purpose. It's how a fantastic new concept or strategy conceived by a select few becomes widely embraced.

It's also how pockets of savvy fresh thinking overcome cultures of indifference or negativity in difficult times and situations. Long-term success will elude an organization that does not know how to scale up what it does well. *"Good is Not Good Enough,"* a game-changing approach for business expansion, is a must-read for all business professionals. Businesses must pursue a strategic route in order to retain organizational excellence.

With this organizational excellence manual, go on a journey that leads to significant performance gains and the creation of a positive culture where everyone is prepared to succeed. It is possible to learn how to build a wonderful organization.

- What is the key goal that your team is attempting to achieve?
- What do you hold in such high regard that you are unwilling to make concessions along the way?
- What does quality mean to your consumers, and how do you quantify it? Are you and your colleagues cultivating great customer relationships? Are you impressing your customers to the point that they will actively and enthusiastically tell others about you?
- Is everyone in your team completely focused on the task at hand? Are you making strides in the right direction?
- Do you have a solid strategic strategy in place?
- Are you using the Pareto Principle of Leadership Excellence to your advantage?
- Are you able to quantify all of this?

The author demonstrates how to develop a successful team and organization step by step in his friendly and articulate way. He provides us with the structure, language, and method so that we have not just knowledge and understanding of the actions necessary, but also the means to carry them out. Contemporary organization might be the most important invention of the twenty-first century. Organizations have carried out plans to send men to the moon and safely return them, to implement the Internet and other communication systems, to discover oil through deepwater drilling and fracking technologies, to deploy lifesaving medical technologies to remote areas around the world, to provide clean drinking water where none previously existed, and to continue to improve the quality of life in emerging markets and economies. This instrument, which you call the organization, has performed incredible accomplishments that would have been impossible for a person to achieve. However, as businesses expand, so do the obstacles and complications they face. External environments are more global, fast-paced, and disrupted by new technology, which organizations must navigate.

Consider a corporation that brags about its happy and engaged workforce. Consider how well this firm will fair if it is revealed that an executive has been permitted to remain on the job despite genuine complaints of sexual harassment or any other ethical violation. Under the weight of the hypocrisy, the shaky foundation that supports the myth of a wonderful corporate culture crumbles. In today's post-# MeToo world, finding innovative ways to combat workplace harassment, prejudice, and ethical breaches is more crucial than ever. A company's claim of having a great workplace culture is incomplete until it addresses these concerns.

While much has been written about employee engagement, climate surveys, and the introduction of Ping-Pong tables as tools to build a healthy culture, little has been written about how important conflict prevention and resolution are to a company's ability to provide employees with an environment in which they can thrive. This book tackles the subject head-on and proposes a novel and new way to decrease, if not eliminate, workplace drama. This book is for the leader, the aspiring leader, or anybody who needs to deal with workplace drama. A reoccurring topic in the book is that achieving the objective of a drama-free workplace will take each of us individually.

Summing Up

The best results are produced when there is an organizational culture that aligns and motivates people. *"Good Is Not Good Enough"* examines the impact of cultural excellence on achieving organizational excellence in both the Indian and global contexts. The book gives the necessary tools for attaining a deeper understanding of the key drivers of organizational excellence. The author explores how to: excite and engage people; address problems that have a direct impact on your bottom line. The book covers the numerous characteristics of organizational leadership and the implications they have on important outcomes such as employee behaviour, work satisfaction, and innovation. It presents a measurement instrument that may be used for organizational culture evaluation, selection, and training, as well as developing strategies to exploit organizational leadership's behavioural aspects at the personal, team, and organizational levels. The book will be useful to business leaders since it tries to suggest some practical solutions for firms to improve their current processes. "*Good Is Not Good Enough*" is a must-read guide for all business professionals. Contemporary organization might be the most important invention of the twenty-first century. The author demonstrates how to develop a successful team and organization step-by-step in his friendly and articulate way. He provides us with the structure, language, and method so that we can carry out the actions necessary to run a successful business.

CHAPTER TWO

BUSINESS TRANSFORMATION

To Achieve Excellence, Fundamental Changes Are Required In Business Operations

"In a world that changing really quickly, the only strategy that is guaranteed to fail is not taking risks." -Mark Zuckerberg

The term *"business transformation"* refers to significant changes in the operations of a firm or organization. This includes personnel, processes, and technology. These modifications allow organizations to compete more effectively, become more efficient, or implement a total strategy shift. Business transformations are large-scale adjustments that companies undergo in order to achieve more than incremental gains in terms of change and growth. However, even organizations that have completed significant changes may not necessarily reap the full financial rewards of their work.

As a result, we looked more closely at the various stages of a transformation's life cycle to see where value is lost and what firms can do to retain it. According to the research, three key transformation activities are particularly predictive of value capture, and firms that have completed successful transformations are more inclined to follow the exact methods that support them. Nonetheless, the findings show that even effective organizational reforms fall short of their full potential. Respondents who reported success believe that their firms received only 67% of the maximum financial benefits that their reforms could have brought. Respondents from all other firms, on the other hand, claim to have captured an average of just 37% of the potential value. Similarly, many organizations might enhance their timing; even those that have completed successful transformations could have benefited from doing so. It might imply maximizing the company's potential through unleashing the potential of personnel, repurposing intellectual property and proprietary technologies, or becoming more efficient.

Business transformations are multi-year efforts that necessitate substantial changes to the changing company's core characteristics. Given the project's scale, breadth, and timeline, it requires leadership from the top—whether it's the CEO or the Board of Directors—to position the organization for long-term success and development. Previously, these transitions took several years. Because of the necessity of these modifications and the help available, the timetables have been expedited. Switching to new business or operational models is one example of a broad and strategic scope. Business transformations are carried out in order to provide value to a company. By implementing business transformation basics into their organizations and the products they supervise, product management can act as an inspiration, a testing ground, and a momentum-maintaining cheerleader for bringing these ideas into reality. The innovative thinking that goes into the produced items might be equally as important as the inventive thinking that goes into the company's operations. Any established company that wants to maximize performance, increase efficiency, and stay in business in five or 10 years should look into business transformation options. There will always be areas, procedures, and structures that might be improved, and ignoring these improvements in favor of the status quo is often short-sighted and harmful. Business transformation may be many things when it has a broad reach. There are several ways to categorize business transformation activities, but they usually fall into one or more of the categories.

This transformation is concerned with the *"how"* of completing tasks and may involve agile transformation. It usually entails a lot of process improvement and automation in order to focus on higher-value tasks. This is usually a continuous endeavor, beginning with the more prevalent ways and progressing to those with lower returns. The ultimate objective is to free the corporation from these responsibilities so that it may innovate or deliver higher-value services and products to the market. Information, data, and digital transformations—Focusing these transformations on leveraging technology to generate more value is the focus. It might come in the form of new, more efficient ways of gathering and exchanging data such as a digital CRM system or online ordering. It also includes harnessing technology and data to deliver new goods and services in the end, both by using technology to develop, produce, and distribute them more quickly and by incorporating digital assets into the new offers themselves.

Many changes rely on changing resource allocation. Organizational change begins with an assessment of how to staff various departments as well as the structure of those divisions. Companies can find possibilities by looking at in-house talents and expertise, how staff are employed, and the various reporting systems. These possibilities might indicate a need to simplify or expand in order to attain more development and success. Breaking down silos, flattening the organization, and right-sizing the headcount are all possible goals. Top-down bureaucratic hierarchies aren't always the greatest for supporting speedy decision-making and adapting to new events as organizations strive for growth in competitive marketplaces. While changing the management structure (removing middlemen, etc.) is a part of the answer, enabling individuals to make their own decisions or swiftly find a consensus is considerably more important. This necessitates knowledge sharing and socializing as well as the establishment of clear communication routes and general organizational openness.

Cultural transformation is, in some respects, the most difficult aspect of company transformation. Corporate cultures tend to develop spontaneously, influenced by the personalities of executives and how they are rewarded and acknowledged. Changing a company's culture takes far longer than other types of transformations, in part because it's more difficult to transfer ideas and intentions into action and practice. When it comes to the subject of managerial transformation, it likewise seldom happens in a vacuum and has a considerably greater success rate. Success requires a clear vision, dedication to that goal, and practice confirming it. Surprisingly, few studies have attempted to quantify what makes a corporate transition successful. The authors examined multiple global companies that had undergone transformation. Author discovered that transformation is more difficult than expected; successful companies shared a common focus on initiatives that prioritized employees, such as DE & I programs and support for women managers' careers, in addition to competitive pay and access to health care. Business transformation has long been seen as the holy grail of the business world—something that is constantly sought for yet impossible to achieve. When John Kotter made his now-famous statement that 70% of business transformation programs fail more than 25 years ago, he emphasized the problem.The latest McKinsey study on transitions reveals that success is elusive and requires a complete strategy. However, some acts are more likely to lead to the realization of the financial rewards at stake. The results of McKinsey's latest global survey, which builds on 15 years of original McKinsey research on organizational transformations, underscore an enduring truth: the more transformation activities a company performs, the better its prospects for success. However, success is the exception rather than the rule. Despite the fact that you've known for years that a holistic approach to organizational transformation is more favorable to long-term change, the average success rate has remained stubbornly low. Less than a third of respondents (all of whom had been involved in a transformation in the previous five years) feel their firms' transformations were effective in terms of both boosting organizational performance and sustaining those improvements over time. Setting effective and ambitious transformational goals is insufficient.

People must comprehend what these goals imply in terms of their day-to-day occupations and what they will be required to accomplish differently. If they don't understand how they fit into the transformation, their behaviors and work processes will remain unchanged. However, the survey findings imply that there may be a perception gap: top executives are approximately 20% more likely than other workers to perceive that their transformation goals have been modified for relevant personnel across the firm. The most successful organizations, according to the survey, are more likely to involve employees and engage them in face-to-face communication, specifically, line-manager briefings (cited by 65 percent of successful transformation respondents), leadership town halls, and a cascade of information throughout the business (for more on employee communication and engagement).

Every company can see transformation as a means of gaining a competitive advantage. In their field, companies with strong brands, good personnel management, and ethical business practices will stand out. Because it comes with the territory, human resources is in a unique position to help others through organizational transformation. As you transition to a new organizational paradigm, use this information to help workers overcome their aversion to change.

In a corporate setting, what does organizational change imply? Organizational transformation (ORG) is a strategic method of getting your organization from where it is now to where it needs to be in the future, according to ORG. In many circumstances, this transition is necessary to address a long-overdue problem or change. Enhancing the adaptability, agility, and efficacy of organizational processes and workflows. Organizational transformation aligns with business goals and can aim at a variety of things, including: Digital transformation, for example, entails keeping up with and being at the forefront of technology advancements. By lowering the time and expense of executing activities, any firm may gain a competitive edge by implementing and employing the correct technology. The capacity to be nimble and sensitive to industry, technology, and workforce trends, as well as pivot when necessary, is required while transforming a business. To move everyone from point A to point B while embracing key principles that make it distinctive, the corporate culture must be adaptive.

For instance, an organization may discover that it has a reputation for high employee turnover as a result of unmanageable workloads. Rather than allowing this pattern to continue, the leadership team and human resources team decide to embark on an organizational transformation process that includes a complete overhaul of all job roles as well as the implementation of new technology to streamline tasks. The united effort makes the company more successful and productive, as well as a better environment for workers to work in. For a variety of reasons, organizational transformation is essential. It is inextricably linked to organizational success and, as a result, to business outcomes. Because every business goes through cycles of development and change, now is a good time to assess how the company is performing and develop a strategic plan for the future. The following are some of the important areas that organizational change has an influence on: How effective are your company's antiquated hierarchy and processes? This is frequently the area of business that requires the greatest reform in order for the organization to reach its full potential. According to a Deloitte study, *"53 percent of leaders feel that transitioning to team-based working has resulted in considerable performance improvement."*

Is your company culture a true reflection of your employees', customers', vendors', and community's experiences? If not, what can you do to change your company's culture and align it with its core values? Human resources may detect areas of concern like high employee turnover, low engagement, and diminishing work quality by analyzing key HR data. High staff turnover, poor engagement, and diminishing work quality may all be addressed with a cultural reform. In order to prosper in uncertain times, a company must focus on having a revolutionary influence on the market it serves. Setting a high standard in terms of how the firm accepts its social duty and prepares personnel to take on a brighter future is one example of this.

"Those who lead by example and demonstrate passion for what they do make it much easier for their followers to do the same." --Marshall Goldsmith

Many corporate executives are considering organizational change. Managers that are on top of their game are continually seeking ways to improve their organization's efficiency and culture. This work is especially important at times of transition, such as the one we've been through as a result of the epidemic. It's also at this point that organizational reform becomes a determinant of long-term viability. Organizational transformation strategies can provide your company with continuity and opportunity at the crossroads between stagnation and sustainability. Any sort of transformation has an impact on your staff first and foremost. As a result, HR plays a critical part in the process.

What does a successful organizational change entail? Kurt Lewin, a German-American psychologist, developed the basic Change Management Model, which defines three stages of organizational transformation that promote success. During the unfreezing stage leadership generates the notion that change is required to better the company at this point. This may be accomplished in two ways: (1) recognizing the need for change, and (2) encouraging new behaviors to replace old ones. Human resources are critical at this phase in finding and communicating data signs of transformative need. Low employee satisfaction and excessive turnover, for example, may indicate a need for cultural change. This drives change based on profitability and productivity when it is supported by management. Adapting At this point, the organization has overcome any resistance to reform. Old undesirable behaviors are replaced by new desired actions.

Organizations frequently endure leadership changes and departmental adjustments, and hierarchies are dismantled. A specific change action is carried out, with role models, specialists, and mentors on hand to guide staff in the right direction. In this stage, training for new ideas and technology is common, pushing everyone to learn new concepts and take a step into the future.

Human resources plays a key role in preserving clarity, conveying change, and dealing with any opposition. The organizational transformation process is complete after the changes have settled and become the norm. Changes in behavior are integrated with a new set of values and expectations by all leaders and workers. Managers and human resources collaborate to help workers who are having problems. The new organization appears to have a promising future. The role of corporate executives and human resources in the development of a company How can leaders and human resource experts assist in the change of an organization? According to research, leaders and HR play a critical role in fostering long-term transformation. Eighty percent of HR practitioners agree that top or senior management is required for successful organizational change.

Transformation does not occur in a vacuum. Instead, it must be a comprehensive strategy that covers several aspects of the business in order to be effective. For example, if your objective is to alter your processes to make them more agile and collaborative, you'll need to think about how it will affect your organizational structure, the technology you're using, and whether or not there will be a skills gap. When going through organizational transformation, Genuity employed this strategy to acknowledge the job done, the reason why the work was done, and the meaning of the work for each employee. Make a list of the steps you'll need to take to alter the company. Begin with the end-results in mind and work your way back through the organization. The transformation process is made easier with a strategy that includes a timeframe.A strategy with a schedule helps to make the transformation process more real and keeps the focus on the task at hand. Transformation does not occur in a vacuum.Instead, it must be a comprehensive strategy that covers several aspects of the business in order to be effective.

"I believe you have to be willing to be misunderstood if you're going to innovate." --Jeff Bezos

For example, if your objective is to alter your processes to make them more agile and collaborative, you'll need to think about how it will affect your organizational structure, the technology you're using, and whether or not there will be a skills gap. When going through organizational transformation, Genuity employed this strategy to acknowledge the job done, the reason why the work was done, and the meaning of the work for each employee. Make a list of the steps you'll need to take to alter the company. Begin with the end-results in mind and work your way back through the organization. The transformation process becomes more real with a strategy that includes a schedule, which aids in keeping the process on track.Let's imagine you want to increase your employee experience, performance, and productivity by X% by switching from obsolete workplace technologies to more current, efficient platforms. Preliminary tool research, RFP submissions, vendor demos, selecting and purchasing the correct tool, integrating it, and onboarding your workers to utilize it would all be part of your timelined strategy. It's difficult to make all of the necessary changes all at once. Instead, prioritize the issues you wish to address first, such as deploying three new workplace technologies one by one rather than all at once.

It's also possible that the transformation strategy will evolve over time. Reevaluate things, adjust the plan, and don't be scared to reprioritize in such scenario. It's critical to include important stakeholders in the process if you want to succeed. At the start of the process, identify who these people are and remind them why the transformation is taking place and what their role is in it. *"Effectively defining roles and duties may result in a 70% boost in transformation success,"* according to one study.

Make the modification process as transparent as possible. Not just to key stakeholders, but to everyone in the organization. It will be less difficult to overcome any resistance to the change. Create a documented communication strategy that covers all issues, including the new company's appearance. Ensure that communication is two-way, that it is a discussion, and that workers have the opportunity to ask questions and express their concerns. You could, for example, hold a town hall meeting or even brief 1-on-1 meetings.

It's critical to have complete agreement with all executives on the objective and extent of the change that has to take place. If there is a dispute, put it on the table, work it out, and adjust the plan as required. Just don't wait till the modification is complete. Employees are at the heart of your business. Focus on their requirements throughout the transformation process and keep them updated on the progress. This can also imply removing dysfunctional hierarchies that obstruct development and rearranging teams, as Accenture did with one of their clients. Employee-centricity will help you gain employee buy-in and boost the likelihood of success during organizational change and beyond. It will help you figure out how much work you've already completed, how much work you still have ahead of you, and whether or not you need to pivot. Utilize data, get input from workers and consumers, and monitor the success of this long-term transformation. The metrics you use to track your success are determined by your objectives.

If, as in your example, you're trying to update your workplace tools, you may track software uptake as well as improvements in employee experience, performance, and productivity over time. Organizational change, when done correctly, leads to increased performance and a business culture. The process of organizational change, on the other hand, can be lengthy and difficult. That is why, in order to thrive, organizations must break it down into smaller chunks, create goals, and have a clear vision and plan, all while concentrating on their staff.

How can a company become a fantastic place to work? Many firms aspire to this, but few have a clear understanding of the effort required to make it a reality. My HR strategy has been very basic for the previous five years: build an environment where people want to work. It's a lot simpler to say than to accomplish. Making the required adjustments requires a lot of effort and dedication, and it may be unpleasant. In a recent piece, it has been emphasized the importance of taking the time to map out the company's intended culture as a cornerstone to becoming a wonderful place to work. These are the four key areas to focus on as part of your journey to creating a great workplace.

Summing Up

Business transformations are large-scale adjustments that companies undergo in order to achieve more than incremental gains. These modifications allow organizations to compete more effectively, become more efficient, or implement a total strategy shift. Organizational change begins with an assessment of how to staff various departments as well as the structure of those divisions. The author discovered that transformation is more difficult than expected. Success requires a clear vision and dedication to that goal, and practice confirming it. People must comprehend what these goals imply in terms of their day-to-day occupations and what they will be required to accomplish differently. Organizational change is inextricably linked to organizational success and, as a result, to business outcomes. Human resources may detect areas of concern like high employee turnover, low engagement, and diminishing work quality by analyzing key HR data. The organizational transformation process is complete after the changes have settled and become the norm.When going through organizational transformation, Genuity employed this strategy to acknowledge the job done, the reason why the work was done, and the meaning of the work for each employee. Transformation does not occur in a vacuum. Instead, it must be a comprehensive strategy that covers several aspects of the business in order to be effective. Organizational change, when done correctly, leads to increased performance and a business culture.

CHAPTER THREE

SUSTAINABLE EXCELLENCE

The Future Of Business In A VUCA World

"I really do encourage other manufacturers to bring electric cars to market. It's a good thing, and they to bring it to market and keep iterating and improving to make better and better electric cars, because that's what's going to result in humanity achieving a sustainable transport future. I wish it was growing faster than it is."- Elon Musk

Can you perform 50 push-ups in a row? Let's shoot for 55 this time and 100 in two months! And if you're who you say you are, give us more than 100 in two months because that's how we push the envelope here! When all three tasks are successfully completed, an environment for excellence is established in that gym because each and every member is very inspired to do their very best because that's the value that defines you. That's who you are. Know exactly how you are doing at the moment and where you want to be in the specified future, and push the limits of every actionable goal along the way. You must use the same logic in your businesses and organizations.

Every business should have a well-defined mission that is reflected in the corporate culture. For example, if your objective is to provide the finest customer service in your sector, everyone in your organization should keep this in mind while they go about their everyday tasks. Leaders in your business may set a good example by acting in accordance with your organization's cultural values. Good-to-great leaders grasp three key realities when it comes to getting started. First, starting with who allows you to more quickly adjust to a rapidly changing reality. If people board your bus because they think it's going somewhere, you'll have a problem when you're 10 miles down the road and realize you need to change directions because the world has changed. However, if people board the bus mostly because of the other wonderful individuals on board, they'll be far faster and smarter in adjusting to changing circumstances.

You should also evaluate each member of your team on a regular basis to ensure they are living up to the corporate ideals you have established. People don't want to get stronger in most of the companies here because no one rewards them for being strong or punishes them for being weak most of the time, no one defines exactly what being strong or weak means, and they don't know how much they are lifting and how much they should be lifting because everything is ambiguous. Their team leaders do not provide them with a vision worth striving for, nor do they establish practical targets in the middle. Everyone is completely befuddled and mired in mediocrity. In this way, your country's cycle of mediocrity is maintained, and you must break it. Excellence, like so many adjectives in the English language today, is frequently hijacked in business contexts to be identical with a desired objective, such as perfection. True, excellence is connected to perfection in its most basic sense, but the two are not synonymous. Perfection is defined as being free of flaws or defects; faultless. According to Psychology Today, perfectionism in the workplace may be the ultimate self-defeating tendency. It makes people slaves to achievement while keeping them fixated on failure, dooming them to a lifetime of doubt and unhappiness. It also has the unintended consequence of weakening accomplishment in the modern world.

When firm executives pursue or expect excellence in their business, whether on purpose or not, it is sometimes regarded by the ranks as perfection. One source of this misperception is the plethora of Power Point presentations that describe what is necessary in order to achieve greatness but seldom reveal how. Only the quality of the output and the frequent target of strikes are presented, and it is up to the ranks to figure out how.

Excellence, on the other hand, is anything different that confers exceptional worth and value, such as a performance benchmark. Excellence is something to aspire towards and is frequently recognized with prizes. Whereas perfection is fixed—it's either faultless or devoid of flaws and defects, or it isn't—excellence is a journey that is more dynamic in nature. Excellence may be defined and assessed in terms of what, how, and by whom, establishing baselines for minimal standards while allowing for creative execution. Rather than a single aim to achieve, achieving greatness is a process to be followed. You may cultivate your own attitudes to perform with an attitude of excellence in all you do, whether or not it is a fundamental value of the organization. The best part about working in an excellence mindset is that you can work within your comfort zone, apply creativity and innovation, and contribute to the organization's success. This, in turn, results in occupational satisfaction and fulfilment. Although CEOs and organizations can set the standard for excellence, it will never be met unless it is customized and implemented at every level of the organization. You may discover the same thing in each of these dramatic, astonishing, good-to-great company transformations: there were no miracle moment. Instead, each organization, its executives, and its workers were kept on track for the long haul by a down-to-earth, pragmatic, committed-to-excellence method — a framework. In each case, steady discipline triumphed over the short cure.

Is your workplace a place where employees feel at ease and encouraged to do their best? An uncomfortable workplace atmosphere may sap your employees' motivation, resulting in low morale and significant staff turnover. To make your employees feel appreciated, make sure your workplace has appropriate lighting, comfortable office furniture, decent ergonomics, and spaces for them to hang out on breaks without bothering their coworkers.

Also, keep the office clean. However, keep in mind the social and environmental elements. Ensure that your employees are acknowledged for their achievements, that they are regarded as colleagues rather than subordinates, and that they have the resources they need to execute their tasks efficiently. To put it another way, they create a social environment in which they can thrive. Employees who are healthy, especially those who have a high overall sense of well-being, are more likely to perform well at work. And, of course, when an organization's personnel work effectively together, the result is great organisational performance. A well-developed corporate social responsibility programme, which is vital for every firm that cares about its employees and its reputation in the community, includes an employee wellbeing effort. However, a wellbeing effort is more than just a wellness programme. Instead, it will address your people's health, social, community, professional, and financial requirements. A suitable benefits package, a comprehensive compensation scheme, and wellness activities are all factors to consider. To promote continued action, inducements, effective communication, and policies will all be employed.

Mergers and acquisitions did not lead to success. There was no press release, announcement, rollout, or anything to promote good-to-great transformations. Rather, they were the consequence of persistent, tenacious efforts that appeared totally ordinary—even boring—to onlookers both inside and outside the organization.The industry didn't matter: Some good-to-great firms focused on unglamorous sectors and nevertheless managed to create excellent outcomes. Every corporation seeks organizational excellence, yet many business executives are unable to identify how to accomplish it. It has always been remarked that *"change is a constant in business,"* but this is especially true now from a marketing standpoint with the increase in digital transformation projects. There is no one-size-fits-all solution to achieving organizational excellence; instead, a multi-channel strategy to enhance and optimize corporate performance is required. Defining your Hedgehog Concept is a crucial step in the process of going from average to excellent. But comprehension and insight don't develop instantly—or even after a single off-site meeting. The good-to-great organizations took an average of four years to develop their hedgehog concepts. It was a cycle repeated over and over by the right people, infused with brutal facts and guided by the three circles. It was an inherently iterative process, consisting of piercing questions, vigorous debate, resolute action, and autopsies without blame—a cycle consisting of piercing questions, vigorous debate, resolute action, and autopsies without blame. The chicken within the egg is this.

Companies that go from excellent to great don't have a label for their transition, and they don't have a program. They don't whine or complain about a crisis, and they don't create one when none exists. There is no evidence that money and change mastery are linked. And although fear does not motivate change, it does encourage mediocrity. Acquisitions can't spur greatness either; two mediocre companies don't make a great one. Technology is crucial, but it only comes into play after the transformation has already occurred. Finally, spectacular results do not come from dramatic processes—at least not if you want them to persist. A genuine revolution, one that feels like a revolution to the people who are experiencing it, is exceedingly unlikely to result in a long-term jump from excellent to exceptional.

Understanding your company's mission is the first step in building an effective organization. Once this is accomplished, you will be able to more clearly define your long-term objectives. Following that, objectives that will assist you in moving toward your goals might be developed. These objectives can then be allocated to people inside the organization so that each one is completed by a specific person or team of people. This responsibility is critical to ensure that your company's plan is implemented. The importance of information is crucial to the success of any modern company and cannot be overstated. Develop metrics that will allow you to track the effectiveness of all aspects of your business and discover strategies to monitor them. For example, you may request that your marketing department measure their monthly website visitor increase in Google Analytics so you can evaluate how successfully their efforts are driving visitors to your site. Most significantly, you may monitor progress toward the goals outlined in *"Strategic Direction"* above. It is vital to note that in order to have a balanced approach to performance, your measurements should be evenly focused on sales, operations, and people/culture.

Once you've set your strategic direction and determined how you'll assess progress, you'll need to make sure that critical messages are communicated throughout your business. Consider your plan for expressing your values and expectations to individuals at all levels of your organization. Email? What about meetings and training sessions? Or how about disseminating information via the workplace intranet? To reach everyone, you may need to employ a combination of these strategies. Whatever communication medium you employ, keep in mind that communication should always be two-way. Allow your employees to provide feedback on business policies and discuss suggestions for change. Indeed, encouraging grass-roots communication is critical. Effective grassroots communications enable problems to be handled efficiently at the lowest possible level, rather than escalating up the management levels.

Effective recruiting strategies minimize employee turnover, lower recruitment expenses, and increase efficiency. Take the time to define the ideal attributes you are looking for in new workers to ensure you pick the right people. These traits will be determined by your company's culture as well as the abilities required in your firm. For example, if your firm is in need of IT expertise, you must prioritise this in your hiring procedures. While talents are crucial, cultural fit is crucial.

Organizational excellence requires trust. Establish trust among all members of your business, from entry-level employees to senior managers. Encourage your employees to express their issues openly so that they may be handled as soon as possible. Nothing builds trust more effectively than clear communication followed by fast and deliberate action. Allow your staff to take action without seeking assistance or direction from their managers. To encourage this proactive behaviour, ensure that all of your employees have the resources they need to address problems, like access to client records or the ability to use modest amounts of company assets without seeking permission. Also, ensure that your policies promote empowerment. By actively encouraging workers to participate in choices that affect their work, you can instil confidence in them and demonstrate that they are valuable parts of your business.

Professionally, give chances for your employees to strive for excellence in their work. However, give them the opportunity for personal development as well. Good examples include assisting people in developing better money management, parenting, and community service abilities. Providing chances for your employees to acquire new professional and personal skills may boost retention and productivity, allowing you to keep a more highly trained and motivated team.

It would almost be impolite not to include Google in a list of firms with a strong culture. For years, Google has been associated with culture, and it has set the standard for many of the perks and privileges that startups are now recognized for. Free meals, staff vacations and parties, cash bonuses, open lectures by high-level executives, gyms, a dog-friendly atmosphere, and other benefits are available. Google employees are regarded as being ambitious, talented, and among the finest in the industry. Maintaining a consistent culture throughout Google's headquarters and satellite offices, as well as among the many departments inside the firm, has proven difficult as the company has grown and spread out. The greater a firm grows, the more its culture must evolve to accommodate more people.

The more a firm grows, the more its culture must evolve to meet the increased number of people and the demand for management. While Google continues to receive high marks for compensation, benefits, and promotion, some employees have noted the growing pains that come with such a large firm, such as the stress that comes with working in a competitive atmosphere. If company culture doesn't allow for a proper work-life balance, hiring and demanding the best from people may quickly become a source of stress. Like Google, Facebook is a firm that has experienced explosive growth while also being associated with a distinct corporate culture. Many similar organizations, including Facebook, provide a lot of food, stock options, open office space, on-site laundry, a focus on cooperation and open communication, a competitive environment that stimulates personal growth and learning, and outstanding perks. Facebook, like other organizations, has the same challenges: a highly competitive market leads to a stressful and competitive workplace. Furthermore, a loose and organic organizational structure that works well for a smaller company does not function well for a bigger one.Facebook has established conference rooms in different buildings, plenty of outside roaming areas for breaks, and managers including CEO Mark Zuckerberg working in the open office space with other employees to tackle these problems. It's an attempt to create a flat organizational culture by promoting equality among competitors through the use of buildings and space. Adobe is a corporation that goes out of its way to give its workers difficult assignments and then gives them the trust and support they need to succeed. While Adobe offers the same advantages and privileges as any other modern creative firm, its culture rejects micromanagement in favor of trusting people to achieve their best. Adobe goods are linked with creativity, and the individuals who make them can only be fully free to create if they are not micromanaged. Adobe, for example, does not utilize ratings to determine staff skills since it believes that this restricts innovation and negatively impacts teamwork. More than anything, managers take on the role of coach, allowing employees to create goals and decide how they should be evaluated.Employees are often offered stock options so that they feel they have a share in the company's success and may benefit from it. Adobe's open workplace culture includes ongoing training and a culture that encourages risk-taking without fear of repercussions.

Many of these businesses have comparable perks and bonuses, but these do not entirely determine the culture. The way employees are treated, as well as the amount of ownership and trust they are given, is an important aspect of business culture. One word of caution: concentrating solely on business culture at the expense of other workforce issues (safety, rules, regulations) might lead to abuses or create uncomfortable circumstances for employees. Even the strongest cultural examples on this list have critics. Always keep in mind that the finest culture makes all employees feel safe and welcome, never isolated or uneasy. Focusing solely on *"cultural fit"* makes it tough to acquire and welcome workers who aren't part of the company's current culture, even if they'd be a valuable addition and fantastic counterweight. If your corporate culture is causing you to have a homogenized staff that thinks and acts the same way, it has to be changed.

Summing Up

Excellence is frequently hijacked in business contexts to be identical with a desired objective, such as perfection. Perfectionism in the workplace may be the ultimate self-defeating tendency. CEOs can set the standard for excellence, but it will never be met unless it is customized and implemented at every level of the organization. An uncomfortable workplace atmosphere may sap your employees' motivation, resulting in low morale and significant staff turnover. Consider your plan for expressing your values and expectations to individuals at all levels of your organization. Allow your employees to provide feedback on business policies and discuss suggestions for change. Establish trust among all members of your business, from entry-level employees to senior managers. Encourage your employees to express their issues openly so that they may be handled as soon as possible. Allow your staff to take action without seeking assistance or direction from their managers. The more a firm grows, the more its culture must evolve to accommodate more people. Like Google, Facebook, Adobe are firms that have experienced explosive growth. Many similar organizations provide a lot of food, stock options, open office space, on-site laundry, and a competitive environment. The company culture makes all employees feel safe and welcome, never isolated or uneasy.

CHAPTER FOUR

VALUE REORIENTATION

Determining How An Organization Is Operated And It's Influence

"It is impossible to escape the impression that people commonly use false standards of measurement — that they seek power, success and wealth for themselves and admire them in others, and that they underestimate what is of true value in life." — Sigmund Freud,

Whatever a small business appears to be on paper in the beginning, the leader or founder might be the most intriguing element of that organization, which no one supporting them should ever take for granted. Solution providers trying to force their views, thoughts, and attitudes on a firm is something Author has seen far too frequently as a client and now as a consulting partner. Of course, that solution provider was selected for their competence, but not at the expense of the firm or the leader's culture.

Even if things are a little bumpy within the organization, it is always crucial to study and watch how it all began and how it is surviving with the person who was there from the beginning. If you believe the culture needs to change, whether at the request of the leader or because you've noticed enough to talk about it, you must construct the other three components alongside that change, not separately from it. If one isn't viable (for example, new technology investments), you'll have to put in more effort into people or processes to overcome it. You are convinced that the combination of leadership, strategy, customers, measurements, workforce, operations, and results will get you there. Leaders and teams that want to see their companies succeed must refocus their efforts and reevaluate their goals as rapidly as possible, going from being *"simple generators of products or services"* to *"value deliverers"* for their customers and other stakeholders. This transition necessitates a mentality motivated by a shared corporate purpose, which should be backed up by an ever-improving management system. The main issue with industries is the high rate of turnover and the high expectations that employees have for their careers. It is critical for every firm to keep its personnel motivated and engaged. Employees can be motivated in a variety of ways since everyone has different goals, but the organizational values and culture are the ultimate motivators for all employees. It's a simple question with a simple response.

When an organization's basic principles are clear, its employees know who they are and what they are a part of. Employees will be motivated to join and work for a company that shares their personal fundamental beliefs. These people will put in more effort because they are passionate about what they are doing and for whom they are doing it. Having a high-performing workforce is conducive to business success. Strong, shared values transform an organization into a hologram in which each component holds enough information to convey the entire organization in a condensed form. By monitoring one person, whether it's a manufacturing worker, a front-desk receptionist, or a senior manager, an observer may gain insight into the whole organization's culture and ways of conducting business.

Hiring, engaging, and growing personnel is heavily influenced by an organization's development trajectory, culture, values, and leadership team. An organization's ideals are its foundation. Strong roots are required for the formation of any organization. Even if the company has high value, it will not expand and thrive unless it has the suitable environment (culture) in which to do so. Organizational values are distinct, and defining them effectively necessitates the ideal atmosphere for them to flourish.True principles and the correct culture are what attract talent to an organization and drive people to stay with it. Simply posting values on a website and in an e-mail signature will not help an organization retain top talent unless its promoters, leaders, and other stakeholders live up to the specified principles. When an organization's ideals aren't given the space they need to be put into action, the culture becomes poisonous. As a result, such a culture has curtailed talent's career / affiliation with the company.

The given views/thoughts are mostly applicable in an Indian subcontinental setting, while certain components may have worldwide relevance. The author draws on his personal experience to provide what is essentially an observational kaleidoscope of organizational behavior. The purpose of this book is not to pass judgement, typecast, or categorize organizations. It makes no recommendations and is merely an attempt to expand on a thought process that is already prevalent in corporate circles and attempts to develop an outstanding culture in the organizational environment.

For several decades, pursuing excellence in all company operations and processes has been a core corporate goal. Corporate planners associate excellence with increased productivity, lower costs, and increased profitability. Excellent organizations, it is often assumed, can weather economic changes, market shifts, and human attrition efficiently (with minimal harm). While the COVID-19 pandemic has not spared the largest conglomerates in terms of financial setbacks, it has prompted several well-run companies to reflect, recalibrate, and reinvent to fit into a changed world scenario in which excellence may well prove the all-important differentiator between successfully weathering economic upheaval and simply surviving.

This is because, while other firms were downsizing, reorganising, and accepting reduced revenues and margins in 2020, great enterprises were considered to have defied the trend and, in reality, to have effectively exploited the crisis as a chance to advance. This has revived the discussion about the value of pursuing excellence as a meaningful, desirable objective connected with the organization's long-term mission.

The purpose of this book is to comprehend the mechanisms that drive excellence as an organizational culture and how it should now be regarded in light of the coronavirus epidemic. To begin with, "good" enterprises must be recognised for what they are. Good businesses are usually well-run, efficient organizations with above-average financials that increase stakeholder value. So, what distinguishes an exceptional company from a good one? Superlative performance in all business operations is a vital objective for an amazing firm. It promotes a culture of *"going the extra mile"* as a habit, making it second nature to all of its employees. It promotes the aphorism *"do it right the first time, every time"* as a basic organizational attitude. A good firm, on the other hand, examines first to determine if the work output is satisfactory before trying for higher performance. This might be the overall industry standard or a standard that is only adequate to meet the set aim. For example, in the case of a product specification, it may be a needed parameter range, or in the case of a customer, the maximum time permitted for delivery, and so forth.

In the process, mediocrity in performance may suffice in many circumstances. I.e., good becoming better is regarded as a positive outcome. What is lost is the vital component of aiming for the *"best"* or *"better than the best,"* which is a fundamental component of greatness as a human activity. As a result, good firms rely heavily on somewhat above-average yet efficient executors. These performers will inevitably be a modest but vital component of the workforce. The Pareto principle will be well proven here, with 20% of the workforce performing 80% of the productive work that has a significant influence on organizational income. Not unexpectedly, the majority of the company's revenue will come from 20% of its clients. Organizations that prioritise excellence as a fundamental value, on the other hand, will have more genius executors than just effective ones. More significantly, they will consistently and superbly perform even when under pressure, with minimal resources, and when all odds are stacked against them. Excellent organizations will automatically develop extraordinary crisis managers who thrive in situations that are out of the ordinary, need deep innovation in thought and practise, and depart from the established SOP.

As a result, business process methodology is constantly reinvented, with productivity actually growing after each crisis. The internal philosophy of these firms is to *"challenge the boundaries,"* whereas the former is frequently to *"limit the challenge"* after the targeted goal is completed to a certain degree. When it comes to product creation, excellent organizations will almost always do it based on need (or market demand). For example, if a client/market conforms to a specified product standard, the firm is required to satisfy it in order to compete in the market. Excellent firms, on the other hand, will envisage tomorrow's market today, i.e., look forward and produce a product that can take over the market in the future through unique creation and R&D (from the ground up). They will be technological leaders who will steer the market in their preferred path. Good firms are generally followers who, seeing the potential offered by the leader, take a *"me too"* approach to goods and business. What must be emphasized here is that brilliance comes at a cost and is supported by strict work discipline and systematic execution. Organizations that swear by perfection operate on the 100 percent concept, which states that every single default or deviation necessitates a complete revamp of systems and procedures. The primary organizational idea is that greatness is founded on good work technique that allows for performance repeatability. Because of this emphasis on accuracy and consistency of top-tier performance, good businesses are frequently viewed as being either sales-driven or technology-led. Other functions, including production, logistics, and procurement, must, of course, toe the line in order to stay on track with the bigger corporate goal.

Despite the trauma caused by the epidemic, many strong organizations retain their distinctive capabilities in industrial processes, strategic sourcing, and financial management. To get off to a good start in terms of excellence, they would need to promote it as a key cultural value inside their enterprises, much like a safety culture, equal opportunity, or gender equality. The difficult element of driving excellence is that it demands shaking people out of their comfort zones (particularly those who have previously achieved the requisite outcomes) and allowing them to experiment with novel ideas. But, again, COVID has always been about ushering in a new normal. The coronavirus epidemic has opened up vistas of new methods of functioning successfully and inspired employees to be imaginative as well as optimise existing approaches.

Most good businesses would be OK with a top management specialist spearheading excellence initiatives. This will entail rethinking strategy, implementing new formats, brainstorming, training/retraining sessions, and so on. COVID, on the other hand, has seen organizational innovation evolve from the ground up, and the time may be perfect to return to making this attempt a ground-level activity that penetrates the layers. Much like the Japanese automakers of the 1970s and 1980s, who pioneered groundbreaking shop floor programmes that substantially enhanced efficiency and set new norms of manufacturing excellence, Consistency is what elevates a mediocre performance to the level of brilliance. When the strength of human tenacity is paired with the necessary knowledge and skill set, the recipe for success in terms of greatness is delivered. Even MNCs that faced existential crises as a result of the pandemic did a deep dive to re-evaluate their fundamental competencies and encouraged workers at all levels to think outside the box in order to sustain morale and seek new meanings for their different positions within the firm.

It is generally observed that organizations and workforces that persevered in the face of adversity, learned new skills, and communicated with one another on a regular basis not only survived the worst of the pandemic, but also created substantial value that has the potential to last in the long run. Workforces infused with (or who imbibed) the fundamental philosophy of constancy of excellent performance set the standard for their particular enterprises. Whether it was a procurement department that, despite material availability, economic uncertainty, and logistics issues, bought cost-effectively on a regular basis, adding considerably to the value chain. Alternatively, a quality assurance department with fewer people might still ensure that consistently high quality standards are maintained at the lowest possible cost. Client-centricity has recovered the spotlight as part of excellence initiatives, with firms understanding that in difficult circumstances, customers seek regular providers to work closely with them and for out-of-the-box solutions that ensure cost advantages on both sides in cash-strapped times.

COVID has emphatically stated that the employee is still the most crucial gear in the organizational wheel and the focal point of all excellence initiatives. While technology and automation have taken the shine off of organizational growth in recent years, the focus is now, and properly so, on human resources. Companies' HR functions have quickly rebalanced to become people-centric again, rather than system-centric in the past. All of this raises the fundamental question of excellence, stemming from the intrinsic human drive for perfection and for doing things correctly. As the old adage says, *"If an activity is worth performing, it is worth doing well."*

Long ago, there was a story about a Japanese baseball club team travelling the American continent. The squad journeyed from city to city, playing a series of matches, losing more than they won against talented American club sides. One feature of the Japanese team's behaviour, however, stood out and was consistent throughout the tour. When the Japanese team finished a game and it was time to leave the stadium, they would willingly take 10 minutes off to clean their dressing room — lockers, tables, drawers, benches — to restore it to the exact perfect form in which they walked in earlier in the day. A curious scribe asked the squad the purpose of this behaviour near the conclusion of their journey. The squad members were noticeably surprised that such a question had been posed in the first place, and their reaction was, *"Someone took the time to make us comfortable by providing us with a spick-and-span changing room."* The very least we can do is repay the favour. It was the most natural thing in the world for them to clean up (and clean up properly!) after usage, and to do so with the same attention and commitment that they put into their game. Let us strive to make greatness a habit that will sustain companies in difficult times.

How can you assure the pursuit of greatness in light of today's society, particularly the unsettling culture that is forming? People who produce and consume, as well as your own personal ideals, strategies, culture, and business principles are all important considerations. Technological advancements are used to benefit processes and people, responsible resource management, society, and the environment. Having a clear vision that is supported by the shareholders and shared with the team, being aware of the business and market dynamics, capturing opportunities, mitigating threats, creating competitive advantage, and finally, building the foundation of efficiency and effectiveness of any strategy implementation, which are related to: Teamwork that is skillful and entrepreneurial, as well as value-based decisions They are the cornerstone of the company's survival. Values are key components that guide our decision-making and shape an organization's culture. Organizational values are a collection of basic ideas or moral concepts that guide people's conduct in organizations. The values of the organization are those who will help leaders and their teams with decision making and the tradeoffs that occur while we are developing a vision and implementing plans. Urgent action is required to raise awareness, and this process must undoubtedly begin at home, where these principles and values must first be developed and reinforced in a citizen. Organizations also have an essential educational function with regard to their employees, suppliers, and consumers, as well as in informing governments about ethics, justice, and values. All of this will necessitate the formation of *"conscious businesses,"* which are those that have conscious people at all levels of their organization, shaping the organizational culture to be more balanced, just, and human, and whose vision, values, culture, and processes will generate meaning and value for their stakeholders on a continuous basis.

Strategic planning entails not just thinking about the future, but also acting on it. In the world, we are seeing the emergence of a society in which values are deteriorating. Urgent action is required to boost the degree of consciousness growing, and this process must undoubtedly be strengthened from within. Strategic planning entails not just thinking about the future, but also acting on it. A major issue with strategic planning that is implemented in organizations is that it should challenge people to think about the future and especially to model it, but it frequently ends up becoming an exclusive tool of analysis of the present, whose activities are usually developed centrally, in a bureaucratic and apathetic manner. Peter Drucker stated that the most likely future *"is one in which you believe, shape, and do the required and sufficient steps to construct it."* So the destiny of mankind is fundamentally dependent on whatever path we choose to take and how we act to achieve excellence.

The vision is a strong tool for pushing individuals out of their comfort zones, producing a creative tension that is the energy that comes into action when we define a goal that is at variance with the existing reality, as mentioned in Peter Senge's book The Fifth Discipline. Creativity reminds me of the need to create an atmosphere in which honest mistakes are acknowledged and used as a source of learning, and where differences are respected and cherished, for it is through them that creative thought is developed. On the other hand, seeking consensus means that everyone participating in the process will give in and lose something. On the other hand, valuing all means that everyone involved in the process will give in and lose something. *"Unanimity is stupid."* Seeking unanimity implies that everyone participating in the process will give in and lose something. On the other hand, valuing all differences and creating something new from them generates purpose and value for everyone involved, and everyone benefits.When there is a lack of freedom, the human mind becomes more inventive. Expect the constraints to be given to the business environment in the form of indicators or trends; it may be too late to react; the crisis must be created. A vision that shifts the corporate level creates creative tension, which creates a positive crisis.

Mapping trends, opportunities, and threats is vital for developing a strategy plan, but the challenge is that they are generally rather powerful signals and hence are clearly detected by all rivals. What competitive benefits might be anticipated from a strategy based on these signals and trends? It must go deeper, and it is critical to pay attention to the faint signals, which are indicators of changes that are likely to occur but are not yet visible. It must also look beyond the company's current market to discover what other industries can teach it. It is also critical to identify uncertainties that have the potential to harm or change the foundations of the firm. And, given this set of uncertainties, determine which of the two or three crucial ones are. However, how does it organise a strategic planning process and the development of corporate strategies in times of increasing frequency and severity of change?

In the current environment, with the globe more connected as a result of the digital revolution, through social networks and mobile connectivity everywhere and at any time, Decentralized and unstructured information is emerging. How do you assemble this collection of data into a strategic plan that makes sense for shaping the future and providing meaning to stakeholders? Author has utilized a series of techniques in multi-departmental workshops that have proven effective: Competitive intelligence is used to map megatrends. Diagnosis, Prioritization, Idea Generation, and Change Management are all hats. To construct prospective scenarios, critical uncertainties must be identified.

Identify opportunities and threats in each prospective scenario, correlate with the strengths and weaknesses identified in the current state diagnosis, and generate strategies and tactics, determining which support is required for each point of attention.

Crowdsourcing to map megatrends and provide future vision fragments, addressing specific themes that represent the previously established aim to be reached as previously defined by the business owner. A narrative description of a future vision told by someone who has travelled to the future and returned to the present to report on what he has seen. Change management entails mapping the drivers of change resistance and developing an action plan to counteract these factors. Determine the level of preparation for the change.

A vision that does not stem from a plan is only a fantasy. To make it a reality, it is necessary to coordinate the vision's construction through a project roadmap and oversee each project's implementation. Every project must have the following components: scope, responsibility, a to-do list with a beginning, middle, and end, as well as the right allocation of resources. It is also critical to create a management ritual to monitor the evolution and possible course corrections. Megatrends are events that drastically alter the way people think, manage, purchase, create, socialise, communicate, and so on. Before the workshop sessions, they should be mapped using competitive intelligence tools. You may use them to identify opportunities and risks that need to be addressed. SWOT analysis is a strategic planning technique that is widely used in the corporate sector. However, all organizations are looking at the same megatrends, with the exception of companies that have a great idea of differentiation. There is a high probability that companies have been looking for the same opportunities and threats and, at the end of the day, are going to compete for the same things in a *"Red Ocean."* The *"Six Hats"* method is used to construct a diagnostic by gathering the strengths and weaknesses of the current state using the first three hats:The colour white is associated with facts and data collection.Black is associated with issue identification, dangers, critical judgement, and the flaws of the organization.The goal of this hat is to collect information on the organization's strengths and key capabilities.The Blue Hat is constantly used for prioritising and project planning; the Green Hat is used to create the vision as well as the generation of ideas for strategic projects; and finally, the Red Hat is used to map the issues of change management: mitigating the detractors' effects and enhancing the facilitators for project roadmap implementation.The *"Six Hats"* approach developed by Edward de Bono is a group discussion methodology employing colourful hats that establish a natural discipline, including parallel thinking related to the concepts, helping the group to think together more effectively.

Consider two people attempting to solve an issue without being aware of this dynamic; the first person's method of thinking is largely black hat, while the second is yellow hat. The person wearing the black hat will argue, *"See, how we have this difficulty, that risk, and that point of weakness,"* whereas the one wearing the yellow hat will disagree, stating, *"See, we have this opportunity, we could achieve this benefit, we have these strengths."* Who is correct? Who is incorrect? Both are correct and incorrect; the beauty of this strategy is that at a given point in the dynamics, everyone is wearing the same hat, harmonising such circumstances and driving us to think in a different way. Both are correct, but the beauty of this strategy is that at a given point in the dynamics, everyone is wearing the same hat, harmonising such conditions and pushing us to think with a new part of our brain that we are not accustomed to utilising, and this will extract fantastic ideas from the process.

The uncertainties are change factors that connect alternative and opposing universes, diametrically opposed worlds, and this separates them from the megatrend, which is something that will happen sooner or later, to a greater or lesser extent, and has only one direction. Crucial uncertainties are those that have the most influence and unpredictability in the industry or company and have the potential to affect the normal flow of operations. They serve as the *"raw material"* for defining the framework of potential situations. Thus, if two uncertainties are considered crucial to the business, four scenarios are formed by combining two by two of each of the uncertainties' diametrically opposing poles. If three significant uncertainties are specified, eight potential scenarios are constructed.

In practise, dealing with two important uncertainties allows for the development of a solid strategic strategy. More than three key uncertainties in their exploration do not provide cost and value. If it were required to employ the features resulting from more than three significant uncertainties, two or three uncertainties might be combined and transformed into one uncertainty until two or three critical uncertainties are found. In practise, dealing with two important uncertainties allows for the development of a solid strategic strategy. More than three key uncertainties in their exploration do not provide cost and value. If it were required to employ the features resulting from more than three significant uncertainties, two or three uncertainties might be combined and transformed into one uncertainty until two or three critical uncertainties are found.

The SWOT approach was used in each of the situations that were generated. The big difference here is that because the uncertainties that have been set are critical for business and, depending on the direction that it will follow, could change the business strategy profoundly, with this methodology, it doesn't matter what this trend is, because the organization has prepared for it all prospective scenarios generated by the combination of uncertainties. Crowdsourcing is the act of gathering ideas and collecting contributions from a diverse set of individuals via an online community in order to produce solutions to a particular problem.

Storytelling is the capacity to convey relevant stories, in this case about a future vision. This approach, as well as all of the data gathered from the other tools, is then used to construct a picture of the future, describing each point of the aim stated by the business owner. This story depicts the future of the company and organization in 20 years.This temporal dimension has psychological significance because it is not a very small amount of time in which individuals will not offer anything out of the ordinary. This time dimension has psychological significance because if it is not a very short period of time, people will not propose anything out of the box, because change would not be feasible in this period of time, and if it is too far, the proposals will have little meaning, because people will not be present to see this reality materialise. Furthermore, the process dynamics have the capacity to engage individuals and, more importantly, keep the organization compromised with the strategic plan's implementation. This effect is caused by the following factors: because the teams were involved in the description of the vision through the concept of crowdsourcing, they felt like co-owners of the story, which has a power multiplier by the ease of communication and also because it stirs the collective consciousness of the organization.

As with the industrial revolution and the internet, we are on the verge of a new breakthrough. The smart object age will usher in the new era. New enterprises will arise from this tipping point, and the traits that organizations must apply in their culture in order to surf this new period must be nimble. New firms will emerge from this tipping point, and the features of these organizations that want to ride this new period must include nimble methods to reinvent and evolve their business, goods, and services while striving for perfection in customer experience. This operational style is more akin to startups, which includes characteristics such as speed, flexibility, and a willingness to take calculated risks in order to capitalise on possibilities that appear on the horizon. This trait is best articulated by the effectuation idea, which suggests a mix of learning by doing and trial and error, built on four pillars: acceptable losses, strategic partnerships, exploitation, and an uncertain future.

Large companies will find it difficult to navigate this terrain because their success has been built on developing processes and procedures that are structured to ensure repeatability, but those who can create an environment with isolated spaces where internal startups can be protected temporarily from old paradigms and structured processes until they can be generated will have both united agility in capturing new business and the ability to perpetuate it.

As you have seen in this book, it is critical to invest in the awareness of people who will shape the organizational culture into a more balanced, just, and human one and whose vision, values, culture, and processes will be used to create meaning and value for its stakeholders in order to ensure the search for excellence continues. Furthermore, in times of change, it is critical to decentralise the development of corporate strategies, raising the level of commitment at all levels of the organization while orchestrating the harmonious implementation of these strategies. Finally, to achieve extraordinary results, resilience is essential.
Leadership, culture, and the pursuit of greatness: In theory, every business strives to achieve excellence, some more than others. Where businesses truly differ is not in their pursuit of greatness, but in how they build strategies to achieve it. There are three ways to consider. While some businesses will attempt to implement two or three of these techniques, only one will often become their major emphasis. Organizations strive for greatness using a conventional approach, an aggressive approach, or a constructive approach.

Managers that follow the conventional approach think that the best approach to achieving excellence is to create a set of systems, policies, procedures, and regulations that control every decision made in the firm. It takes years to build and define these. The ultimate objective is to safeguard everyone in the company against their own shortcomings. This swiftly devolves into safeguarding the organization from individual shortcomings. There are additional regulations governing which decisions managers may and cannot make. To cover every eventuality, several layers of management must be established, resulting in a cumbersome organizational structure in which decisions are continually pushed *"up the ladder."* This motivates managers to use passive-defensive leadership strategies, which leads to the formation of a passive-defensive culture. There are passive-defensive cultures in which everyone is urged to comply, push choices up the chain of command, and resist change. People advance by being pleasant, according to the rules, and avoiding accountability.

Although the initial purpose was to strive for greatness, this gradually morphed into one of sustaining the status quo. Employees are disengaged in organizations with a passive-defensive culture, as evidenced by high turnover and/or excessive sick pay. The service and product quality are always subpar at best and sometimes sub-par. An aggressive approach is adopted by managers who, like the preceding managers, have a basic belief that people would not perform effectively if left to their own devices. They, on the other hand, believe in deeds rather than words. Managers here utilise an aggressive-defensive style, requiring employees to work long, hard hours and never make a mistake. They micromanage with an autocratic style that is always looking for defects and blunders.

This strategy produces an aggressive-defensive culture in which mistakes are not tolerated, individuals compete with one another rather than collaborate, and everyone is driven to work long, hard hours. This method can produce short-term results. In the long run, however, service and product quality are irregular at best. Employee turnover and burnout are high. Simply recruit tyrants as managers and hold everyone responsible for learning on their own and generating outcomes, no matter the cost. As previously said, in the quest for perfection, this method might offer short-term results. When the benefits end, the business implements additional aggressive-defensive strategies aimed at achieving results at the cost of their most important resource—their people.

The objective of these new measurements shifts from the pursuit of excellence to the pursuit of perfection—where *"heads roll"* at the tiniest of errors. Individuals in this culture ignore the notion of continuous progress, focus on insignificant details, and push people into a 24/7 dedication to the cause.

Even calculated risks and thinking *"beyond the box"* are abandoned as people try to escape penalties. People advance in their careers by working long hours, never making a mistake, and having the capacity to dominate and influence others. A constructive approach necessitates that the business and its management team recognise that the pursuit of excellence can only be attained when leaders believe in their people and invest time and effort in developing them. They understand that everyone wants to perform well and will strive for perfection if given the chance and resources to do so. As a result, there is a constructive culture in which individual effort is valued, employees are encouraged to take measured risks, and people are held accountable for service/product quality. People are also encouraged to participate in decision-making by offering unique and creative ideas. They are required to treat one another with decency and respect, as well as collaborate and assist others. The end product is nothing short of spectacular. Employees in constructive environments are often engaged, with minimal turnover and sick pay (people are literally healthier in these cultures). They also cite not only excellent levels of service and product quality, but also a culture of continuous improvement. These companies are achieving goals that were thought *"pie-in-the-sky"* and unattainable just a few years ago. The Pursuit of Excellence is expanded to include a persistent pursuit of excellence. Which approach and culture are you looking for? The conventional approach is time-consuming, but it is secure. People know what to expect on a daily basis. They are disengaged yet determined to maintain the status quo and avoid *"rocking the boat."* Staying out of trouble takes a *"back seat"* to service and product excellence.

The aggressive approach is simple to adopt. Leaders do not require training or growth; they only need the power and skill to keep others responsible. This strategy can yield short-term benefits, but it frequently comes at the price of the individuals doing the work. It is typical to have high levels of burnout and turnover. Companies, on the other hand, can adopt measures to compensate for predicted turnover if people are not a valued resource. On the plus side, if the senior management team is hands-on, competent, and prepared to work long, hard hours, this sort of culture may be maintained with infrequent success. They must also be prepared to accept greater stress and the associated stress-related sickness. All of this can be frightening for managers, especially if they feel employees should be handled like children, micromanaged, disciplined, and subjected to a slew of regulations. However, the outcomes of a constructive culture vastly surpass those of other civilizations. The employees are enthusiastic, and everyone strives to give excellent service and product quality. In other words, it ensures the organization's long-term existence and growth.

Summing Up

Leaders and teams that want to see their companies succeed must refocus their efforts and reevaluate their goals. Organizational values are distinct, and defining them effectively necessitates the ideal atmosphere for them to flourish. Organizations that prioritise excellence as a fundamental value will have more genius executors than just effective ones. Excellent organizations will automatically develop extraordinary crisis managers who thrive in situations that are out of the ordinary, need innovation in thought and practice, and depart from the established SOP. Organizations also have an essential educational function with regard to their employees, suppliers, and consumers. More than three key uncertainties in their exploration do not provide cost and value. As with the industrial revolution and the internet, we are on the verge of a new breakthrough. New enterprises will arise from this tipping point, and organizations must be nimble. This operational style is more akin to startups, with characteristics such as speed, flexibility, and a willingness to take calculated risks. Large companies will find it difficult to navigate this terrain because their success has been built on developing processes and procedures that are structured to ensure repeatability. It is critical to invest in the awareness of people who will shape the organizational culture into a more balanced, just, and human one. Managers here utilize an aggressive-defensive style, requiring employees to work long, hard hours and never make a mistake. They micromanage with an autocratic style that is always looking for defects and blunders.

CHAPTER FIVE

DEVELOPING CULTURE

Achieving Organizational Excellence Through Culture Building

"The work environment is very important in determining how enjoyable work is. It is very important to work with smart guys who have a superior level of intellectual bandwidth and still have softer skills as well" –Kumar Mangalam Birla

There is a gap between how you want work done and how it is actually completed. And it is your responsibility as a leader to bridge the gap. Getting culture to permeate the whole business is really difficult. It necessitates a shared knowledge of your fundamental values and the actions that those core values reflect. But what generally occurs? People grin and nod, and then go about their business as usual. Are you too cynical? Consider that you have a completely engaged team that has embraced shared beliefs and habits.

Even if you did, behaviour slips, people go back into old patterns, and you end up with two cultures. You've all seen the one that everyone claims defines your organization and the way employees really get things done. So, how do you go about fixing it? You bridge the gap by eliciting the hidden culture. Talking to your new employees is a fantastic place to start. It might be tough to tell what hidden culture exists in your business since, well, it's hidden. The author discovered that new employees had the most fresh eyes for seeing the disparity between how a corporation claims work is done and how it is actually done. Talk to your new hires and find out what's puzzling them.Enquire about the procedure, then broaden your team's participation. It is not unusual for cultural habits to evolve, and it is acceptable to make behavioural changes without shifting your shared values. You might choose to pave that new path. Sometimes there's a valid reason to steer folks back down the same routes they've already taken. To obstruct either of the newly constructed paths, you may use huge planters or a seat. This ludicrous narrative is now being translated. Your workers will forge their own paths, ignoring your organization's stated cultural rules. You must make a decision. Do you allow for evasion? If you do, the author has discovered that pointing it out, being explicit about it, forging a new road, and paving it will assist you in drawing out your hidden culture. If you don't want the new course to continue, you must make that clear as well. Why is it harmful? Is there anything you can put in the way, like a planter or a bench, to keep people from taking that path? At the end of the day, whether it's hidden or obvious, work is being done in your business. The idea is to uncover your hidden culture.When you know how two people handle things differently, you can typically obtain what you need from the correct individual at the right moment, but this will come at the cost of the entire. You may witness this happening in your own house. The kids understand that they should ask you for certain things, but for others, they should go to mom. They know precisely where their mother is, but you have other objectives, interests, and preferences. This is a low-stakes version of what might be a high-stakes challenge. Misalignment costs more than basic things in your job. It can lead to schisms between functions, confusion across layers, and discord between teams.In both situations, misalignment has resulted in severe financial loss and personnel termination. This high-stakes variant can cost your company money and employees. It also imposes a significant burden on morale and culture. Misalignment in the bottom line leads to confusion and dissatisfaction, and it's your role to keep everyone aligned. Your team cannot just use the same playbook; you must be on the same page. So, how do you encourage alignment? You know they're effective because low-stakes practise leads to high-stakes achievement. And you've seen how these values have borne fruit in my home and at work. Everything is dependent on open and straightforward communication.Isn't it true that it's easier said than done? You must delve deep and get very detailed. Consider your organization's aims. When it comes to sharing objectives, are you upfront and honest? Does your team establish and discuss shared goals on a yearly and quarterly basis? Otherwise, it will be difficult for you to identify and allocate tasks, as well as for your staff to prioritise their projects and time. Consider your roles and responsibilities. Are you honest and transparent about who does what and who is ultimately responsible for moving things forward? Do team members understand their roles and what is expected of them? They probably don't know if you're not talking about it.In bigger companies, you'll need to convey and redeliver a clear knowledge of reporting structures so individuals know where they belong. Finally, consider your unique preferences and triggers. It is also important to be upfront and honest about these matters, both with yourself and with your immediate reports. Your children are more knowledgeable than you about which buttons to press in your home. Identifying your own preferences, personal triggers, worries, and insecurities requires effort, self-reflection, and emotional intelligence. Sharing these with your staff and encouraging them to do the same requires vulnerability.When you take the time to make this effort, you make clear what everyone already sort of understands. By discussing these topics, you inspire individuals to be direct, honest, and honest about themselves. You create a safer workplace where people don't have to walk around on eggshells and aren't subjected to passive-aggressive tensions. When you just take the time to talk about these things, to discuss organizational goals, to define expectations about roles and duties, to disclose your organizational structure, even if it's in flux, and to be honest about your personal stuff, the author discovered, People feel safer once everything is out in the open, expectations are clear, and trust increases.People can advance in Maslow's hierarchy. And as you go up Maslow's pyramid, your team will perform better, get stronger, and generate more. This is all easier said than done. So, before starting another video, take a moment to ponder alignment. Is your team on the same page as you and your vision? Take into account your own objectives, job, preferences, and personal triggers. Have you been honest and forthright with your team? If not, restart the chat.

If you are going to achieve excellence in big things, you develop the habit in little matters. Excellence is not an exception, it is a prevailing attitude. -Colin Powell

Getting where you want to go is heavily reliant on knowing where you are now. You discussed your work style, work-life balance, and how you engaged with peers in the past. Essentially, you have created your own norms and cultural expectations. You were able to appreciate those differences and realise what had worked for each other in the past by discussing them with each other before embarking on a new future together. Now, culture is just how people interact with one another. And, if you set out to create a strong corporate culture, you should begin by honouring the past: the way people used to do things. This will necessitate some sensitivity on the part of the team as they recognize and explain their own cultural expectations. However, by being interested, you will be able to identify and focus on common expectations, both positive and unpleasant. Second, identify potential areas for expansion. People aren't particularly good at knowing what they want. Once, Henry Ford stated, *"If I had asked people what they wanted, they would have responded with faster horses."*

The first area of concentration is a well-defined culture. Your employees should come to work because they want to, not because they have to. The company's goal, vision, values, and behaviors must all be identified and branded. What is promoted, discouraged, tolerated, and rejected is shaped by this cultural paradigm. The definition of a culture needs a great deal of thought and consideration. Once defined, it must become ingrained in the company's DNA. As we began to act on the behaviors we stated we would not allow, trust grew, and workers began to take personal responsibility for ensuring that behavioral concerns were evident. A study published in the Harvard Business Review in 2018 identified eight different types of culture, and it's a fantastic place to star.

"The reasonable man adapts himself to the world; the unreasonable one persists in trying to adapt the world to himself. Therefore all progress depends on the unreasonable man." - George Bernhard Shaw

Your staff will be a lot better at distinguishing between what they've done in the past and what hasn't worked. Draw these concepts so that you may create them with these issues in mind. Write a list of what you want to keep, what you want to get rid of, and what you want to add. List down what your team actually wants to pack on the journey after they've discussed their previous experiences and you've pointed out your team's shared expectations and places for improvement. It's fine to leave some old baggage at the trailhead, especially now that you've acknowledged and articulated it. If you haven't already guessed, this is a team activity. Culture is shared, and the easiest way to inspire buy-in is to create it cooperatively. Are you prepared to begin? Consider the cultural expectations you have from previous work environments and your personal life right now. Make a list of everything.

You may have taken deliberate measures to transform your principles into practise, and you may have made space for employees to practise having fun in specific ways that are still part of their typical work routine. Now, in your organization, you've probably chosen values that you believe are essential, and you want to implant those values in individuals and teams, which may be extremely difficult to achieve well. So, in order to assist, the author would like to give a brief procedure that you may follow to transition from values to behaviours. First and foremost, he wants you to understand what your values mean to your team. Values, such as trust, honesty, and teamwork, can mean very different things to different individuals.And when your team lacks a clear understanding of what each of these truly means to the team, putting the value into practise becomes practically difficult. So, first and foremost, take the time to understand exactly what your team believes about each of your fundamental principles. Following that, you'll need to transform each value into a list of behaviours. This will require some creative thinking. Consider how each value manifests itself in your job. What does it mean to be respectful in meetings, collaborative projects, and the break room? Is it different for clients than it is for staff? And what scenarios are likely to put one's regard to the test? How do tough talk and impassioned disagreements vary while being respectful? Take the time to consider how you intend each value to manifest itself by outlining practical actions that you hope your staff will adopt. Understanding the actions isn't enough. You must now bring them to life in your team. To accomplish so, you must first address the question, what protocols do we need in place to promote, if not assure, that certain behaviours occur more frequently? But it took some time for me to really grasp what you meant. You had to speak with a large number of team members. You have to extend your understanding of the term. And you discovered that, for you, cooperation entails people working together in a specific way. It's about bringing the proper individuals into the room, appreciating different points of view, bringing out quiet voices, and strengthening our listening skills. You mentioned that working groups are an excellent venue to foster these practises. So open invitations for working groups were necessary to get the relevant folks in the room. You urged working group members to spend their first session defining relational ground rules for how they were going to work together in order to foster varied viewpoints, pull out quiet voices, and increase listening. But you weren't finished yet. And neither will you. Organizational values are not as static as you would believe. It is not sufficient to go through this process once. You'll need to repeat this process on a regular basis so that your team understands what your corporate values are and how they manifest in your workplace. Not sure where to begin? You may put the method to the test by using one of your own values. Write out what it means to you, and then make a list of the behaviours you would like to see. Then it's up to you to figure out how to incorporate such behaviours into your current routine.

From Human Resources to Resourceful Humans The need to use human capital has never been greater, with business transformation emerging as the defining phrase for growth executives in the disruption-driven period following the epidemic. Of course, the same development leaders recognize that it is easier said than done if they have not prioritized developing a strong company culture that puts people first in the past. Organizational culture reasserts its impregnable position as a vital business lever in this scenario.

The relevance and role of organizational culture have been widely established in a large body of literature. However, there have been several ways to get there. Execution eats planning for breakfast, as they (don't usually) say. To execute a strong company plan, your whole team must operate in lockstep, led by shared principles and fervor, and aligned toward a common goal. In short, it necessitates the right kind of culture: one that binds your people together and produces the results you desire. In a PWC study, CHROs, CEOs, board members, and experts from a variety of industries were polled.

Organizational structure, according to 59 percent of study respondents, is where the significant transition is taking place. Flexibility was seen as a key development priority for employees by 42% of respondents. 52 percent said they were not confident in their ability to easily redesign organizational structures. ' Unsurprisingly, 33% of respondents said that employee productivity had decreased. The primary aim for today's leaders is to create a dynamic, dispersed, and inclusive organizational design that is fueled by "whole leadership." Do they have what it takes? Their cultural environment will determine how they build, nurture, and scale.

What is the most effective method for fostering corporate culture? Culture does not emerge from thin air. It is everyone's responsibility to plant, water, and inspire it on a daily basis. Culture is a dynamic, living phenomenon. It is based on the active decisions we make every day at work. It differs from other corporate assets in that it appears to a company's employees, as opposed to, for instance, its strategy deck, finance portfolio, or policy file, which might all be passive or inactive parts. Even when they aren't at their most energetic or expressive, people are never *"passive."* Culture is something you can deliberately and actively influence, as it can be recharged and reinforced by purposeful and opportune nudges, incentives, and interventions (rewards and reprimands).

Most people are unaware that culture is continually interacting with and adjusting to its external and internal surroundings, looking for windows and chances to sustain continuity. On the other hand, this renders culture sensitive to powerful pressures and *"impressionable."* As a result, staying "in its lane" becomes a critical priority for leaders. Controlling culture, on the other hand, is easier said than done. While most CEOs are well-versed in strategy and planning, they run into trouble when it comes to culture. This is reasonable because culture isn't something that can be measured with the five senses or quantified on a spreadsheet. It is a (sometimes) mystifying and (always) elusive beast to catch and tame because of its moorings in unspoken behaviour, habits, and standards.

Successful businesses do not happen by chance. They are a result of culture, or a system of shared ideals. Culture does not guarantee success, but it does raise the likelihood of success. Leaders shape the culture as well. Leaders who know how to motivate people, help them realise their full potential, and guide them through challenging situations are significantly more likely to take their firm to the next level. There is no better moment to start if you are a first-time founder and have not yet thought extensively about the type of leader you want to be. Learning the art and science of culture-building is one of the most significant tasks you can embark on. The fact is that everything a founder does, especially in the early stages of a business's growth, shapes the culture of that organization, for better or worse. As a result, it is significantly preferable to be deliberate about the procedure. The following are some of the most critical factors to consider as you work to create a strong, self-regulating culture that will provide your organization with a competitive advantage.

The vision, values, work environment, and internal conduct of a corporation make up its culture. It is your company's individuality. It is in charge of employee perceptions of the firm, the way it works, and the message it conveys to its customers. Why does it stand out? •How is your firm perceived? And what is its reputation? Why is it important to have a strong company culture? You may fail, regardless of skill or resources, if you do not have a solid business culture. If you look at successful firms like Apple, Google, Amazon, or Disney, you'll see that their corporate culture has a common thread. They are aware of the values that their brands represent. What message do they want to convey to their customers? They look after their workers and give them excellent perks and advantages. They appreciate their workers' decisions and collaborate with them in a respectful and trusting manner. In an interview, Steve Jobs, Apple's former CEO, stated that the company has a strong collaborative culture and does not have any committees. He discloses that they are structured similarly to a startup. They have allocated personnel to their various goods and services on an individual basis. Since its foundation, Apple has followed this organizational culture. This demonstrates that Apple was adamant about its corporate culture and how it wanted to operate. They believe in collaborative working, and the company's goal is shared by all of its employees. They believe in their product and are proud of it, which shows in their actions. As a result of its vision and culture, Apple became the world's most valuable technological business. It's entirely up to you how you structure it. Your company's ideals, beliefs, and goals transcend your identity.

This is when you understand that no matter how far your company grows, you will always be a part of it. Use the correct leadership style and concepts to keep everyone on track and to encourage your staff. If providing exceptional customer service or being devoted to your clients is one of your fundamental principles, make sure you reinforce and convey it to your personnel. Your organization's grasp of business structure and behavior is a quality that your organization has. As a result, it's critical to work hard to build a culture that aligns with the company's mission and values. With this method, you'll be able to help your company stand out from the corporate throng. A bad hire may drastically turn the game around for you. Hire people who fit your culture—people who can share your vision and collaborate to achieve it. When you first start a business, you see a lot of possibilities. The first step is to set objectives and work toward them. You establish a strategy, employ people, and work diligently to attain your goals. When it comes to establishing a strong corporate culture, having the appropriate vision is crucial. When doing so, you should also make sure to set reasonable, attainable goals. You cannot have irrational ambitions or make promises to your staff that will never be fulfilled. What does your company stand for? What issues does it address or resolve? These kinds of questions may appear to be moralistic, yet they are critical for any company. It establishes a brand's reputation as well as what it stands for. Coca-Cola claims to revitalize the mind, body, and soul. Coca-Cola stands for this, and it is committed to promoting happiness. Coca-Cola also encourages an inclusive work environment that values the diversity of people, skills, and ideas.

You can't have a great corporate culture unless your people are content and pleased. Ascertain that your staff are happy with their jobs and that they like working with you. Because a workplace is made up of such a diverse group of individuals, it is preferable to conduct an internal job satisfaction survey. A survey may help you analyze and improve your company's culture, as well as increase overall employee happiness. Employees that are pleased and content with their bosses and work environment are more likely to put up their best effort to help the firm succeed. Your employees are the foundation of your business. As a result, it would be beneficial if you looked after your personnel. Make certain that none of your staff feels left out. Pay attention to what they're saying. On their birthdays or work anniversaries, surprise them. Try to get to know them on a personal level, and be open and honest with them. Support your employees and go out of your way to help them when they are in need. You can establish a team that can flourish and accomplish anything if you care about your people and help them grow. It's just as important to keep good individuals as it is to hire the right ones. You quickly recognize that the teams you form have promise and can aid your company's long-term growth. They contribute to the development of your company's culture and are quite useful. On the other hand, keeping these people is difficult. Make every effort to keep them. Please put together the greatest employee retention program you can for them. More importantly, make them understand that it is their firm as well, and that its long-term viability and development are largely dependent on them. Is your company's culture strong? Or do you wish to strengthen your company's culture in accordance with its values? If the answer is yes, then this is how you create a fantastic corporate culture. All you need is resolve to adapt to any unwanted change, as well as tenacity and conviction in your mission.

Strong leadership is the foundation of a strong culture. However, in the early days of a firm, when a first-time entrepreneur is likely to wear multiple hats, it can be difficult to discern what strong leadership truly means in practise. Most young founders have previous corporate job experience, so they understand what it is like to report to a boss. They frequently believe they understand what it takes to be a leader—that management and leadership are synonymous. They are, nevertheless, diametrically opposed. Management is about effectiveness, which is taking something that already exists and making it more efficient. Leadership is about bringing about change and steering people down a new path. Whereas management is concerned with control, leadership is concerned with influence. Management's goal is to gradually improve. Whereas management seeks to gradually guide people toward a goal, leadership may be disruptive, even revolutionary. Leadership is about understanding when and how to break the status quo. No one, in my experience, works for anybody else; you all work for yourselves. There have been several books produced on how to become a more effective leader. However, in my experience, there are three crucial parts of leadership that are easy to ignore, particularly for first-time founders:

Storytelling is one of the most critical abilities a CEO can have—and one that is rarely taught in typical business schools. There is no better way to connect with other people than through stories, whether for fund-raising, acquiring customers, recruiting employees, or motivating employees. Every day, as an investor, I listen to proposals. The pitches that grab my imagination, generate empathy, and challenge me to imagine myself in someone else's position are frequently the ones that resonate the most. Make good use of the CEO's bully pulpit. It might take years and a slew of failures for some first-time entrepreneurs to grasp how intently people listen to every word they say. When you're not used to that degree of attention, it may be unsettling, but it can also be quite empowering. It matters a lot to compliment an employee, especially in front of other employees. With this in mind, praise should be made as public as possible, but constructive comments should always be kept private. The only person you should ever criticise publicly is yourself. In that vein, don't be frightened to be exposed. The capacity of a leader to be vulnerable with his or her team may be extremely important, yet it is a skill that is seldom exercised. Most leaders feel that exhibiting any evidence of weakness is a sure way to get fired. However, there are occasions when displaying vulnerability gives sincerity and a sense of shared humanity. It's tempting to act as if you have the solution to everything. The ability to declare, *"I don't know,"* on the other hand, may play a critical role in establishing a healthy culture—and avoiding costly mistakes. You want your direct reports to be candid with you about their own uncertainties and worries. Everyone understands it's safe to let their guard down when you're prepared to display weakness.That is what builds a cohesive team.

"Culture" may appear to be a hazy notion, yet it has a specific meaning: an organization's common ideals. For better or worse, the principles embedded in a company's culture will serve as a guiding light for how personnel manage anything from a new client to a crisis response. A corporation that has a strong, well-established culture transforms into a self-policing organism. No one needs to constantly look over employees‘ shoulders since a common set of values encourages them to make the right decision. When an organization reaches a certain mass, it is vital to codify its culture. When a firm has expanded to around 20 workers, when it has created clearly defined organizational roles and opinion leaders in key areas, it is time to codify the organization's collective value system. So, what's the deal? because the firm has reached a critical juncture. There is one group of workers that have been with the founder since the beginning. They have a strong feeling of ownership over what they have jointly created, and they are prepared to go to any length to ensure the company's success. These *"first-wave"* startup personnel are typically unconcerned with titles or jobs. They understand that if the firm succeeds, they will be rewarded with a potentially life-changing windfall.

However, at around 20 people, you are now adding a second wave of personnel. These second-wave personnel are less likely to anticipate personally reaping the benefits of the company's success. The title becomes crucial all of a sudden. The role assumes significance. It is necessary to delineate their dominion. If you are not cautious, the second wave of personnel might develop a micro-culture that is significantly different from what the firm has had up to this point. Before they sign on, make certain that the company's culture and principles are enshrined in a written declaration. *"This is how we do things here,"* you should be able to explain to newcomers. Two of the most essential things you must learn regarding cultural codification are: Collaborate with others.

Corporations are not democracies, yet a cultural statement is a communal choice that must be made. If an employee offers your culture statement to a new hire with an eye roll, it's generally because it was a top-down, ego-driven edict from the CEO. Instead, co-author your cultural statement with the company's other important stakeholders. Discuss what makes your culture special and significant. Make a precise, structured statement about your culture. You will not just strengthen buy-in as a result of this. In my experience, you will also benefit from what your colleagues have learned from their previous responsibilities about what works—and what doesn't—in defining an organization's culture.

Make your points clear. It is all too easy for cultural declarations to devolve into a litany of jargon and hazy ideals that have nothing to do with reality. For example, at one of my previous businesses, the company's culture statement said that urgency should be a vital aspect of the organization's culture. But, in fact, what does *"urgency"* imply? A colleague from that business who joined me in my current venture saw that individuals worked 80 hours or more per week to display "urgency." No one was sure what type of behaviour was expected of them. So, working together, we devised a better way to communicate what we wanted our culture to embody: Do now what you may postpone until tomorrow. *"Practice what you preach,"* as the old saying goes. It is equally crucial for a leader to preach what they practise. The most essential thing entrepreneurs can do at times is to advocate and promote the culture they are creating.

You may have noticed a similar thread running across these examples of excellent leadership and culture: effective communication. Communication is always your first and most crucial responsibility as a leader. To do it properly, you must be familiar with the three primary styles of communication. Each has a distinct purpose and should be used in various situations. They are as follows: One-to-many mode to raise awareness and spread information, such as *"this is what we're doing,"* these are your important efforts, and so on. However, when done correctly, one-to-many communication increases your accountability to your team. Consider it more like reporting to your board than issuing edicts. By your behavior, you are telling your workers, *"I work for you, and I am accountable to you."* Many-to-many sort of communication serves as a debate forum, enabling constructive conflict. A well-debated conclusion is frequently a good option. Therefore, you should develop a platform where people may question and discuss. One person will always be authorised to make decisions and be held accountable for them, but they should not do it in a vacuum. The idea is for your employees to not just be aware of a decision, but to also believe in it and feel involved in its success. That can only happen if everyone gets an opportunity to express their concerns, objections, opinions, and recommendations. One-to-one Communication is exactly what it sounds like engaging an employee on a personal level. The purpose here is to foster trust and commitment. You're demonstrating that you care about this person as a person. You are aware of their objectives and problems, and you aim to be an ally in their pursuit of success.

This is not an exhaustive list. There is a lot more that goes into creating a successful culture, and there are a lot of additional questions you'll need to answer to guarantee your business is expanding in the most efficient way possible. However, thinking thoroughly about the culture you're creating—even simply realising that this is a significant question—is a great place to start. The many situational leadership styles, as well as when and how to use them. If you are the first CEO of a new firm, your career as a leader is just getting started. You have a far higher chance of achieving your target if you are deliberate in your actions along the road.

Understanding and development a successful organization must have a culture that is founded on a set of deeply held and broadly accepted ideas that are backed up by strategy and structure. Three things happen when an organization's culture is strong: employees are aware of how top management expects them to behave in each scenario. They feel that the anticipated answer is the correct one, and they are aware that showing the organization's values will be rewarded. The backdrop for everything an organization does is determined by its culture. There is no one-size-fits-all cultural Employees that actually embrace the ideals are rewarded and recognized. Employers play a critical role in sustaining a strong culture, starting with recruiting and selecting applicants who share the organization's beliefs and thrive in that culture; developing orientation, training, and performance management programs that outline and reinforce the organization's core values; and ensuring that appropriate policies and procedures support those values.

Template that fulfills the demands of all businesses since industries and conditions differ substantially. All have agreed on cultural priorities at the top, and these principles are centered on the institution and its goals rather than on individuals. Successful business leaders embody their cultures every day and go out of their way to express them to their staff. Every day, successful company executives embody their cultures and go out of their way to communicate their identities to employees and potential new hires. They are clear about their principles and how those values shape and govern their businesses' operations. See? What does it mean to be a values-driven business? An ineffectual culture, on the other hand, may pull the organization and its leadership down. Employee disengagement, high turnover, poor customer relations, and decreased earnings are all instances of how a bad culture may hurt the bottom line. Culture is a hazy phrase that is commonly used to describe a nebulous aspect of a company. Despite the fact that there is a vast corpus of academic study on corporate culture, no commonly accepted definition of culture exists.

Rather, the literature provides a variety of perspectives on what organizational culture is. Leadership practices, communication methods, internally dispersed messaging, and corporate festivities are all examples of how organizational culture may manifest itself. Given the complexity of culture, it's not unexpected that words used to describe different cultures differ greatly. Some of the terms commonly used to define cultures include aggressive, customer-focused, imaginative, fun, ethical, research-driven, technology-driven, process-oriented, hierarchical, family-friendly, and risk-taking. Methods of hiring procedures that are effective might help a company capitalize on its culture. Hiring has historically concentrated on an applicant's skills, but when a new hire's personality fits that of the organization, the employee is more likely to deliver better outcomes. The financial industry need a fresh focus on culture in order to attract talent and applicants. People pick occupations based on the corporate culture.

In contrast, ill-fitting hiring and subsequent hasty exits cost between 50 and 150 percent of the post's annual salary.Unfortunately, approximately one-third of newly recruited employees depart within a year, voluntarily or involuntarily, and this percentage has been progressively rising in recent years. Check out these 5 interview questions that every recruiter should ask. It might be difficult to find staff who will fit in effortlessly. The most common blunder an organization can make when trying to recruit candidates is to present a false picture of itself. If new recruits realize they have been duped, they will be dissatisfied, most likely leave, and morale will suffer while they are still on the job. Another disadvantage is that individuals are more hesitant to take unpleasant measures towards those who are similar to them. As a result, mediocre employees who share similar cultural values are more likely to stay in their jobs. Similarly, while an organization's comfort level is visible when its culture is aligned, too much comfort, according to experts, may lead to groupthink and complacency. During onboarding, newcomers are taught the company's value system, standards, and required organizational behaviors.

Employers must assist newcomers in integrating into the organization's social networks and ensure that they have early employment experiences that promote the culture. Employers can utilize these programs to push workers to perform in ways that are consistent with the company's culture and values. If cooperation is a key value, incentives should be focused on teamwork rather than individual accomplishment. Employers can also highlight individuals who best represent the company's ideals. Employees who work in environments where there is a lack of cohesiveness and similar goals outperform those who work in environments where there is a lack of cohesion and similar goals.

Performance management systems may have a significant impact on company culture by explicitly articulating what is expected of employees and offering a feedback tool that informs employees about right behavior. Conflicting signals about company culture can breed distrust and cynicism, which can lead to, or aid in the justification of, activities as harmful as embezzlement. Cultural discrepancies, according to experts, can lead to workers being frustrated, believing management is deceitful, doubting assertions from higher-ups, and being less willing to put up their best effort. Organizations may spend a lot of effort and money developing a culture, but they may not see the same results—especially if CEOs, managers, and lower-level workers all have different perspectives on the company's culture. Employers must ensure that the company's culture is communicated to all workers in a clear and consistent manner. In order to build good strategies that support corporate objectives and goals, it's critical to first assess organizational culture. But how do you quantify something as difficult to define as culture? Following the identification of essential elements of culture, such as values, degree of hierarchy, and people and task orientations, companies can analyze culture by following these steps:

Cultural assessments, as well as other activities like cultural audits and 360-degree feedback, can assist in revealing discrepancies. Then, and only then, will leaders be able to erase the discrepancies. If customer service is a component of the company's culture, consider how much time employees spend visiting customers' sites, how much connection they have with customers, what customer service training they get, and other indicators of customer service emphasis. Select start-ups, such as AirBnB and Ola, expand and become dominant forces in a turbulent business climate plagued by hyper-competition, while others stagnate or fade into obscurity. In addition, although some huge corporations, such as Google and IBM, continue to innovate and thrive, others, such as Nokia and Eastman Kodak, stagnate or crumble in difficult times. Clearly, size, age, breakthrough goods, or marketing brilliance alone do not determine the long-term success of new or established businesses.

High values and charismatic CEOs, contrary to common belief, are not necessary. Implementing a long-term and disciplined strategy that encourages customer-centricity, financial prudence, continual innovation, and talent involvement leads to holistic success. Such an approach is necessary for building strong and long-lasting organizations. The process of creating a long-term, non-linear business is comprised of a succession of decisions, actions, learning, and pivots. While the particular procedures differ depending on the business environment, each firm must pass through five crucial phases, or maturity levels. Each maturity level provides new organizational activities while consolidating old ones. The effective execution of essential practices and their disciplined incorporation into the organization's culture are required for an organization's journey across these stages. The book, *"Good to Great,"* lays forth a framework for transforming a good firm into a great one. It contains a really helpful model that ties the theories together in a way that is both memorable and relevant. To develop a decent firm into a great one, you must do everything it takes.

There are signs that it's time for a cultural shift. Culture, like yourselves, is a living, breathing organism that might suffer from illness from time to time. It's crucial to remember, though, that meltdowns don't generally happen overnight; they're the product of a gradual erosion of the values, goals, and forces that have held the team together along the trip. A cultural matrix frequently throws out telltale signs and warning signals long before it reaches the point of disintegration. It is up to culture keepers to be nimble and skilled enough to recognize them and act with the appropriate response at the appropriate moment.

It shouldn't be difficult to spot such threats to your culture and act before they reach boiling point, whether it's an ambitious effort at change that isn't quite going as planned, a merger or acquisition that has left employees confused about the *"big purpose,"* or a bad review on Glassdoor. If you're alert, it shouldn't be difficult to spot such threats to your culture and act before they reach boiling point. In the marketplace, your brand identity is becoming more muddled. And, when you do appear in public debate, it's not for the reasons you'd want.You're losing top talent to your competitors.

Setting a new direction, vision, and strategy for the firm, and then getting employees on board, is often the first step in transforming a company from excellent to great. One of the most crucial aspects, though, is to get the right people on board and to get the wrong people off. To put it another way, get the proper folks on the bus while getting the wrong people off. Then you'll be able to go somewhere fantastic. The proper individuals are readily motivated and require minimal management, resulting in excellent outcomes. Hire folks that have a lot of character. To make a firm great, you need a culture that will work for the employees. It seems less like work when you recruit the right individuals who like working together. You won't need to inspire the proper individuals since they will be self-motivated. It is impossible to achieve a great vision without excellent people. If you have any doubts about employing someone, don't hire them. Keep looking for that special someone.

Summing Up

Getting culture to permeate the whole business is really difficult. This high-stakes variant can cost your company money and employees' morale and culture. The idea is to uncover your hidden culture. Culture is shared, and the easiest way to inspire buy-in is to create it cooperatively. Culture does not happen by chance; it is a result of culture, or a system of shared ideals. Strong leadership is the foundation of a strong culture, but it can be difficult to discern what strong leadership means in practice. Leadership is about bringing about change and steering people down a new path. You must ensure that the company's culture and principles are enshrined in a written declaration before they sign on. Make a precise, structured statement about your culture. Employers play a critical role in sustaining a strong culture, starting with recruiting and selecting applicants who share the organization's beliefs and thrive in that culture. An ineffectual culture may pull the organization and its leadership down. There is a vast corpus of academic studies on corporate culture, but no commonly accepted definition of culture exists. To make a firm great, you need a culture that will work for the employees. It is impossible to achieve a great vision without excellent people. Hire folks that have a lot of character.

CHAPTER SIX

CRITICAL COMMUNICATION

Your Clear Communication During Organizational Change

"The secret of living a life of excellence is merely a matter of thinking thoughts of excellence. Really, it's a matter of programming our minds with the kind of information that will set us free."- Charles R. Swindoll

Managing change might feel like navigating a ship into a big storm that your crew can't see. Have you ever been a part of an organizational transformation that was poorly managed? You thought you took the time in your business to fully think through the substantial change you were making to your organizational structure. You prepared, and you had multiple one-on-one meetings. Yes, you made certain decisions, but you then communicated them to all of the top management. You used a trickle-down technique to disseminate knowledge throughout the business, and you even included opportunities for bottom-up queries and input.Even after all of that, many across teams thought you messed up the transition. Some people jumped overboard, while others called for a mutiny. It's true that it's difficult to please everyone. It's also easy to think that people heard but didn't like the change, or that poor communication wasn't the underlying issue.

Perhaps you can relate. But what did you discover? Change, on the other hand, can never be over-communicated. When you evaluated it, you discovered flaws in your procedure. There are certain things you might have done to make the transition less difficult. You know you have a different perspective on management today. So, how do you keep the crew together while you sail through the next storm?So, according to the first author, you need a tendency toward fast communication. Even if the facts change, providing information as soon as it becomes available and across all roles fosters confidence. What type of communication is required for your team? You must value active communication over passive communication. Face-to-face interactions, small group meetings, and maybe an all-hands gathering are required. Email announcements and weekly memos, as well as displaying information at the water cooler, will not suffice. Change is personal, and you must approach it as such. What are you going to tell the team now? You may have heard that, in the lack of information, people make up their own stories. This also holds true for why. When a company is going through a transition, you must explain why. Context is essential, and delivering what without the why is akin to offering change without context. You must supply both. Without both, the gossip mill is in full swing. How do you turn it off? Both should be shared. Consider connecting your communication to both the forest and the trees. And it's critical to communicate to your staff why the change is necessary for the business, as well as how it relates to your goal and vision. People are really concerned about how the change will affect their job and their position in your business.It's important to remember that communication is a two-way street. You must listen, and listen some more. It's the old *"two ears, one mouth"* adage. How can you provide a forum for people to debate and challenge the changes? You could organize a number of participatory, all-hands meetings. You may need to hold small group meetings with the people who will be most affected on a regular basis. In any case, change is a process that must be communicated and managed over time. It's never enough to just make an announcement. If you're lucky, your team will ask probing questions and raise relevant topics. When the questions start coming, be prepared to listen with empathy.Change may be terrifying. Some people in your company will freeze, others will fly, and still others will fight. It is vital that you pay close attention. Recognize each viewpoint with respect, ask clarifying questions, assume positive intent, and most importantly, avoid becoming defensive. It's tough to overcommunicate when it comes to change. Author hope you can learn from my mistakes as you traverse these treacherous seas. Follow the advice author provided. And, while the process may still have some difficult patches, you'll be more real, transparent, and compassionate, and you'll sail through the tough patches, creating trust with your crew and improving morale.

From the viewpoint of its employees, what makes a firm great? If ever there was an open-ended inquiry, this is it. The possibilities are nearly unlimited, and it all depends on who you ask. However, if I were to answer this issue in a single statement, it would be that excellent employers know how to keep their staff motivated. Employee involvement is critical to a business's success. Only 34% of the US workforce is said to be engaged, costing $7 trillion in lost output. Here are a few examples of how excellent firms cherish and respect their employees. If you follow these steps, you'll be the next firm that everyone wants to work for.

Feedback is really important. It is the key to both trust and vulnerability. But it's more than just soliciting input. Things started to get strange following the request. If you read Kim Scott's *"Radical Candor"* a couple of years ago, it changed your perspective on criticism. She suggests that you close each one-on-one meeting by asking your direct report a simple question. You began asking that question the very next day, and it profoundly transformed how you interacted with each member of your team over the following three months. When you posed the question for the first time, the majority of your team requested you to repeat it and stared at you. Then they'd say something like, *"Nope, everything's OK here."*You can imagine the internal conversation. Giving feedback back was no longer an option you provided; it was now a must, and it worked, kind of. You didn't get a yes the next week. You begin to receive genuine input, such as what the team wants you to accomplish or refrain from doing. Asking for input is simply the first step. After you've asked, you must listen, which might be a challenging job. You'd want to share a few key things you've learned about getting feedback. First, the quality of feedback you receive is proportional to your level of trust in your reports. Some members of my team offered specific suggestions for how you could better assist them with their work.Others remained ambiguous and safe. When you hear the word *"vague,"* ask yourself, *"Does my report feel safe?"* If not, what can you do to build that trust? Creating a secure setting includes all the nonverbal indicators you provide; for example, are you looking straight at the person you're speaking with? Or are you engrossed in your computer? Are you looking at the same thing? Is your body language mimicking theirs? Making these changes will show your direct report that you care about them.Make a safe space for yourself and be prepared to truly listen. Now comes the difficult part. Don't respond when your direct offers its feedback. If your team is anything like mine, your reports will contain difficult-to-hear information. Some of the input will be accurate, perhaps more than you'd like to accept. You'll also encounter certain misconceptions based on insufficient facts, as well as other concepts that simply don't make sense. You'll almost certainly be inclined to take all of the comments personally. Take a deep breath, listen, and refrain from reacting. Remember, you asked for criticism; there's no use in whining now that you're getting it. Finally, be thankful. Make it a point to emphasise that feedback is beneficial. Thank you for being open and honest. For the most stupid or cruel demands, and there will be some, ask for some time to think it over and vow to either modify things or discuss why the change is probably not the best way ahead. The key to navigating this process is to listen for understanding and be prepared to grapple with the comments you hear. This will not only help you and your team build trust, but it will also help you do things that help your team get work done and avoid doing things that don't. If it isn't a win-win situation, I don't know what it is.

"Every step moved in the chess like competition of the world with
Intelligent ideas surely paves the way to achieving excellence
By efforts based on ingenious techniques to see works are done
With efficiency, effectiveness and suitable efforts to complition!"

Creating secure feedback loops and listening carefully are two of the best ways to be clear from the top. Feedback leads to clarity, and clarity aids in the development of connection and trust. Safe feedback loops allow people to communicate truthfully while decreasing the fear of reprisal and the weight of potential wounded sentiments. The formula for building feedback loops is straightforward. Your team requires a method for sharing. It is your responsibility to listen, process, reply, and then listen some more. Creating a safe environment for your employees to discuss might be more difficult, especially if trust has been eroded in your business. Messages are misheard in low-trust contexts.Consider a dispute between friends in which a misunderstanding compounds matters. Consider the same debate between two coworkers who do not trust one another. If you want a healthy culture in your business, you must establish secure feedback loops. As a result, leadership can stay linked to the entire business and take advantage of chances to explain and re-clarify as needed. To begin, conduct a mental audit of your organization. What processes do you have in place to encourage positive feedback within your organization? Consider how higher-level executives obtain accurate information. You're talking about qualitative and quantitative data regarding projects, initiatives, strategy, and culture from lower-level staff. Hopefully, you have a good sense of your own team.What about the members of your team's team? Have you made room to skip level meetings? Do you have access to front-line employees? If not, what can you do to modify these circumstances? Is it necessary for the team to meet in small groups to exchange ideas or provide feedback?

Have you found other anonymous methods of collecting input so that employees who feel less comfortable may still feel like they have a voice? Whatever mechanisms you choose to use, make sure they assist you in creating safe areas for feedback. Openness and communication are required for the creation of successful safe feedback loops. Is your company sharing, listening, and responding in a healthy manner over healthy timelines?Set up processes that will encourage increased transparency and communication if they are not already in place. These feedback loops will assist you in staying in touch with the pulse of your firm.

Because of the magnitude of the problem, time is of the essence, and business is critical to finding a solution. However, corporate strategy must be aligned with a nature-friendly and gender-equal goal that relies only on renewable energy, recovers biodiversity, strives for gender-equal employment practices, and advances toward a completely circular economy. Given the environmental issues we face, the following changes are projected to occur during the next 30 years: Greenhouse gas emissions must be cut in half by 2030, with near-zero emissions by 2050. By 2050, this would imply a reduction in fossil fuel consumption of at least 80%. We are working to end world hunger. We need to generate 50% more food by 2050. Meanwhile, to maintain human and planetary health, the environmental impact and biodiversity loss of that food production must be reduced by two-thirds. To rehabilitate the world's seas, waste sources such as single-use plastics must be eradicated. Other forms of pollution will have to be severely decreased in order to safeguard the environment and human health. By 2050, a near-completely circular economy will have been established.To promote gender equality in the circular economy and environmental governance so that, by 2030, all women and men, including young people and people with disabilities, have full and productive employment and decent work.

It may surprise you how often people with good intentions speak in ways that cause uncertainty and distrust within businesses. Trust, like seeds, requires specific circumstances to flourish. This appears to be fertile soil, adequate sunshine, and suitable watering for seeds. Cultivating trust also necessitates the presence of specific structural features, as well as a healthy atmosphere and open relationships. Every business is unique, but one thing that the author has observed that helps all organizations create trust is by promoting transparency between levels and functions. This implies that frontline personnel and supervisors require some access to high-level executives, and more communication across functions will aid in the development of trust in very significant ways.You got the right people in the room to tackle the difficult problem by involving a variety of levels and individuals across functions, and by valuing all views, you established trust along the way. With group projects, you cross-pollinate teams. You bring together layers of personnel for social gatherings and issue resolution. You also have communications that improve internal communication among workers and volunteers. For building trust through relational equality, these measures are sunlight and irrigation. Working together enhances communication, and communication fosters mutual understanding, which helps the development of trust. Growing trust and openness are dependent on the soil of relational equality. So, how has your company's soil fared? Are you structuring work such that people may communicate with others across levels and functions? If not, now is the moment to make a difference.

Spend time togetherIt takes time to create trust. Your organization's crew has expanded dramatically during the previous decade. Throughout your expansion, you kept a relatively flat organizational structure. While this model kept all employees connected to the top, it didn't allow for much growth inside departments, and cross-functional collaboration was limited. Longevity made internal advancement difficult, and cross-functional collaboration was uncommon outside of our directors. You opted to make the organization less flat in the hopes of addressing all of these challenges. You created a layer of managers, and in your wildest fantasies, you expected this new team to interact and behave similarly to the director team. Hold that thought for a moment. Consider your senior year in high school. What was it like on your first day of freshman year? You knew a few students from each of your classes, but none of your personal buddies were present. A few students spoke up, most of you remained silent, and a few in the rear created a peanut gallery. You were a long way from a group of trustworthy buddies.You had a group of friends after a few months, but it wasn't until your senior year that our entire class came together, mostly around a common concern that all of this was going to end when you were off to college. But four years is an inordinately long time to wait for trust. Compare it to your water polo experience. Your first two weeks were spent on double days before school even started. By the end of it, you were not only in shape, but you also had a slew of pals who had made it with you. After two and a half decades, you could still converse with those men. Why did you expect the group to act as a team in the absence of sufficient training? Your point is this: You must foster shared experiences if you want to speed trust development in your team. Isn't it simple? Perhaps you experimented with a few different types of double days for our new management group, and it took some time to locate the best match. You have a few facts to share as you build your own trust boosters. To begin with, acknowledge that not all time is equal. Next, acknowledge that not all labour is created equal. Your employees will easily distinguish between busy tasks and meaningful work. Group projects that build teams must be challenging and significant, with wicked challenges that your firm must address. Working on these difficulties together will bring up the types of challenges, disagreements, and shared achievements that you experienced. If there is no opportunity to communicate the lessons and influence change, the team will be aware, and the endeavour will fail. So, if you want to increase trust, you'll need to urge your team to spend time together accomplishing challenging but important work.

Because the majority of individuals are not independently affluent, they must work in order to survive. Great employers understand the benefits of providing a decent salary and recognizing employees for their contributions to the team. When employees are underpaid, they may perceive themselves as being underappreciated. These repercussions will be reflected in their attitudes towards the firm, but they are also more widespread. Low salaries, for example, are linked to increased personal stress and disease, both of which can have a direct influence on performance. Great organizations understand that well-paid people are a financial advantage, not a problem.

Great firms give their employees a steady stream of opportunities to learn, develop, and grow in a variety of ways. Mentoring team members is emphasized, with the goal of encouraging them to continually strive for their own best while taking advantage of teaching moments along the way. Why is it so critical for the employer to take the lead in this situation? Because if you don't keep lifting the bar and providing your team with the means to achieve it, you'll find yourself stuck with a team that is continually wondering whether there's anything better, and more fulfilling, out there. Employee feedback is highly valued. Many businesses claim to respect employee feedback, but few actually do. Great firms value employee feedback and pay attention to it.

Smart businesses utilize the review process to keep communication lines open. When an employee receives comments on their performance during a review, they should be allowed to provide input about the firm and their time working there as well. Smart firms also know how to take criticism in stride and never make an employee fear that providing constructive input would result in bad consequences. Give your employees a vested interest in the firm. Here's the deal: Employees are paid to execute a job, and they may be doing a fantastic job at it. But why should they expend more effort if they aren't getting paid?

This is why excellent businesses give their employees a stake in their success. Consider quarterly performance incentives, stock options, or profit-sharing arrangements. Employees that are invested in their firm are more likely to perform at a higher level. Money is a powerful motivator for people to achieve their goals, and it shows them how much they are appreciated. Ascertain that everyone's time is respected. Some businesses make the mistake of believing that your time isn't valued unless you work in a corner office. The fact is that each person of your team deserves to be acknowledged for their time.

Team members should be provided time to work on assignments at their leisure on a daily or weekly basis. This may be catching up on a long-term project they've been neglecting, cleaning or organizing their office or another location they're in charge of, or visiting your company's professional library to brush up on their abilities. Giving employees some autonomy shows that you trust them to utilize their time wisely and productively, which leads to respect.

If you're the sort that likes to micromanage, this may be challenging because it requires you to relinquish some control. You hired these people, however, because you believed in and valued their abilities.Why not demonstrate them by allowing them to experiment with different ways of doing things? For example, rather than following a one-size-fits-all policy, an employee who encounters a dissatisfied client might use their own judgement to improve the situation. Top employers understand that diversity and innovation are what set them apart. Allowing your employees to do their duties the best way they know how would only limit their originality and brilliance, which would be detrimental to everyone.

This should go without saying, but it's important to mention nevertheless. Great firms don't wait till the end of the year to congratulate a team member on their achievements. How would your staff know when they're succeeding if you just told them once or twice a year that they're doing a wonderful job? Talent and hard work can be recognized in a variety of ways. Some firms have an employee of the week or month program, but personal recognition is sometimes the best option. A thank you and a pat on the back are just as valuable, if not more, than their name on the wall.

Employee safety and protection are not a concern for companies that people desire to work for. This entails having a secure work environment and settings that are pleasant to be in. For office occupations, this may entail back-supporting desk chairs and carpeting devoid of snags. Additionally, the company's management consider its employees' emotional well-being. They provide comfortable break rooms with facilities that are within their budget, as well as private spaces for nursing moms or team members who wish to have private chats with one another. Being a wonderful place to work is all about treating your employees with respect and recognizing them as individuals.It's realizing the importance of treating each team member as an equal partner in your company's success. Great firms know how to get things done.

Summing Up

Managing change might feel like navigating a ship into a big storm that your crew can't see. Some people jumped overboard, while others called for a mutiny. When a company is going through a transition, you must explain why. Face-to-face interactions, small group meetings, and maybe an all-hands gathering are required. It's important to remember that communication is a two-way street. People are really concerned about how the change will affect their job and their position in your business. Change is a process that must be communicated and managed over time. You begin to receive genuine input, such as what the team wants you to accomplish or refrain from doing. Make these changes now to show your direct report that you care about them. If your team is anything like mine, your reports will contain difficult-to-hear information. Openness and communication are required for the creation of successful feedback loops. Feedback leads to clarity, and clarity aids in the development of connection and trust. Top employers understand that diversity and innovation are what set them apart. Giving employees some autonomy shows that you trust them to utilize their time wisely, which leads to respect.

CHAPTER SEVEN

COMPETITIVE ADVANTAGES

Creating Attributes That Enable Your Organization To Outperform

"As you progress towards enlightenment you will find that you become a winner at anything, not because you are so concerned about winning anymore. You are just concerned about the pursuit of excellence." - Frederick Lenz

There's no doubt that competition has been fiercer in recent decades. Clients frequently cite it as a critical requirement. Rather than seeing rising competition as a danger, organizations and leaders that want to build a sustainable future through *"competitive advantage"* see it as an opportunity. While leaders have less control over external influences, leadership effectiveness and organizational culture may be affected and improved in the face of increased competition. There are a handful, but many of the world's top corporations have failed, downsized, become outdated, or been purchased by stronger competitors since 1985. In 1985, GM and Ford were the world's two largest automakers, but they spent the next ten years hemorrhaging cash, losing market share, and attempting to turn things around. Wal-Mart, Verizon, banks, and technology corporations ousted venerable industrial firms like ITT, which reorganized and fell out of the Fortune 500. Digital

Equipment and Wang Laboratories, two once-dominant computer companies, have virtually vanished. Even resurgent behemoths like Apple and IBM peered into the abyss of insignificance and made painful reforms before fighting their way back to the top. Successful businesses frequently fall into three traps that cause their glory days to fade. The first is the physical trap, which occurs when large expenditures on outdated systems or equipment obstruct the pursuit of newer, more relevant investments. There's a psychological trap in which business executives become fixated on what made them successful and fail to recognize when something new comes along to take its place. Then there's the strategic trap, which occurs when a corporation is only focused on today's marketplace and fails to predict the future. Some firms are unlucky enough to fall into all three traps. There is solid evidence that when leaders operate as an aligned collective coalition, it may have a favorable influence on a team's and an organization's performance results, as we've seen in organizations. The simplest method to identify your competitive edge is to ask yourself, *"What sets you apart from the competition?"* And, more importantly, why should buyers select your products or services over the competition? The first stage is to define and articulate your competitive advantage, then compare it to your competitors to evaluate whether there is enough of a difference for customers to select your company over others right away. Differentiating your company from the competition might be done through marketable features or cheap operating costs, for example. It ultimately boils down to what your customers desire. Companies are growing and failing faster than ever before as a result of today's rapid technological progress. The following is a list of ten firms that were once the most innovative in their sector, but have since lost their competitive advantage. It's not a Hall of Shame—most of these companies are still viable rivals that might one day innovate their way back to glory. Rather, these experiences show how lost opportunities and tunnel vision can throw even the most powerful companies off track. Many businesses, large and small, may benefit from these teachings.

Recognize what's essential to them. They provide products and services that are specifically customized to their requirements. To be relevant and profitable, you must find and preserve your competitive advantages by consistently analyzing the market and upgrading your products and services. Although many people still refer to it as the Sears Tower, Chicago's tallest structure is now officially known as the Willis Tower, after a British insurance broker who is one of the building's principal tenants. Sears left a long time ago, and with it, the spirit connected with such a historic structure. Sears helped popularize catalogs, marketed many of suburban Americans‘ household items, and created durable, cheap brands like Craftsman and Kenmore. Later in life, however, Sears was caught off guard as competitors such as Wal-Mart, Target, and Amazon ate into its market share. As it sought to regain its footing, Sears dabbled in insurance, financial services, real estate, Internet service, and a variety of other businesses.

It might be a financial catastrophe, a disruptive rival, or simply a case of expansion hitting a brick wall. It could also be the outcome of rigorous future planning. The leadership imperative of the twenty-first century may be strategic change. Huron's Innosight established a system for evaluating strategic activities with the goal of discovering best practices that reflect leadership excellence across sectors. Apple, which completed one of the most remarkable transitions in business history but is now focused on executing its present strategy rather than aggressively entering new growth sectors, is one of the most striking names missing from the list. Here are the top ten organizations from a list of twenty that underwent major transition in 2019.

Determine and choose a market sector in which clients have distinct requirements. It might be anything, such as a particular service or place. If you specialize in a service or product that your competitors don't provide, make it available to your customers. Promote your product's pricing, distribution, and locational advantages and strengths. It is critical to sustain your competitive edge after you have achieved it. Maintaining a competitive edge will be easier with a continuous improvement program. The most powerful competitive edge your company can have is a plan that no one else can duplicate. Competitors might copy a competitive advantage based only on products and services. When companies instead focus on building circumstances for collaborative leadership and participation among workers and consumers, they gain a competitive advantage. A distinctive organizational culture emerges when mission, vision, values, and strategic direction are authentically shared and when people are aligned and engaged. Others have a hard time replicating their essence, or DNA.

Blockbuster This video-rental chain made it through the transition from VHS to DVD without a hitch—until the next big change. When Netflix began shipping DVDs through the mail, cable and phone providers began offering video-on-demand, and Redbox began renting videos for $1 a night through vending machines, Blockbuster was caught off guard. Blockbuster's traditional retail shops appear hopelessly antiquated now that video streams through computers and phones. With a fighting chance of catching up, the company is liquidating hundreds of locations, paying off debt, and emulating some of its competitors' practices. However, instead of leading its industry, it is now pursuing it. Netflix has had a string of successes.Netflix: Founded in 1997, Netflix has evolved from a mail-order DVD business to a prominent streaming video content service, as well as a leading supplier of original content. It has received several international honors for its own shows. In terms of revenue, Netflix is the seventh-largest internet firm in the world. Adobe is putting its money on digital experiences. This San Jose-based computer software firm expanded beyond its core of creative and document tools to include digital experiences, marketing, commerce platforms, and analytics, while switching from packaged software to cloud subscriptions.

Dell had a different notion back when IBM and Hewlett-Packard still sold most of their goods through stores: cut out the middlemen and sell straight to consumers. When the Internet came along, Dell took off, and competitors were left reeling as they tried to keep up with its soaring sales. However, Dell began to struggle a decade later as mobile devices began to supplant PCs, low-cost Asian machines slashed profits, and large clients began to expect end-to-end service, not just hardware. Dell has responded with mini-laptops, cellphones, and other popular items, but it is currently lagging behind.

No business marketed the camera as effectively as Kodak did for over a century, with advances such as the Brownie camera in 1900, Kodachrome color film, the handheld movie camera, and the easy-load Instamatic camera. However, with the arrival of digital photography and all the printers, software, file sharing, and third-party apps that Kodak had mostly missed out on, Kodak's illustrious reign came to an end. Since the late 1980s, Kodak has tried to diversify into pharmaceuticals, memory chips, healthcare imaging, document management, and a variety of other industries, but the magic has never returned. Its stock price is currently around 96% lower than when it peaked in 1997. A "Kodak moment" indicated something worth storing and enjoying a generation ago. Today, the word has become a corporate bogeyman, warning executives that when disruptive technologies encroach on their business, they must stand up and respond. Unfortunately, as time passes, the nuances of what occurred to Eastman Kodak are lost, causing management to draw incorrect inferences from the company's troubles. *"It is not the strongest of the species that survives, nor is it the smartest of the species that survives. It's the one that can adapt to change the most."* Charles Darwin said it best. Eastman Kodak, a long-time leader, declared bankruptcy in 2012. Blockbuster Video went out of business in 2013. In 2011, Borders, one of the largest book shops in the United States, went out of business. Why did these once-great-brand-name enterprises eventually fail? It's because they haven't been able to adjust to change. Furthermore, they were unable to unlearn and relearn. Let's talk about the significance of transformation in this context.

Microsoft It was essential in bringing the PC to a wider audience, and it continues to dominate most of the software business. But, like Web TV, e-books, cellphones, and the tablet PC, Microsoft has mishandled or passed over numerous wonderful concepts that others have seized on. "How come none of this was commercialized?" Govindarajan inquires. "Execution is the issue." It's dangerous to stick to one business line, especially in a fast-changing market like technology. And indeed, the market is moving away from the PCs on which Microsoft's software is built.

Motorola's first great success was with automobile radios, which led to two-way radios, which led to the world's first mobile phones being built and sold. Motorola controlled that market until 2003, when it released the popular Razr, the world's best-selling mobile phone at the time. However, Motorola neglected to focus on smartphones that could handle e-mail and other data while newcomers such as Research in Motion, Apple, LG, and Samsung quickly gained market dominance. Motorola was defeated so quickly that its mobile phone sector became a chronic loss leader, prompting the corporation to announce plans to spin it off into a new company this year, leaving the main Motorola to concentrate on networking equipment and a few other areas.

Sony controlled the market for TVs, cameras, video recorders, and many other consumer electronics not long ago, and the Walkman was as widespread as the iPod is now. However, as Sony grew into a multibillion-dollar conglomerate with film and music divisions, it lost control of several of its key product lines. The shift from hardware to software, which focused on the brains of the gadget rather than the circuitry, threw Sony and some of its competitors off. As a result, faster-moving competitors such as LG, Samsung, Vizio, Apple, and different cell phone manufacturers—which, of course, also have cameras—have caught up to this old-school innovation.

Sun Microsystems is a company that makes computers. It's only a matter of time before luck strikes again. This computer company started developing high-end servers just as the computer revolution was getting started, and it realized the benefits of networking and universal software that could run on any machine. Sun's Java programming language, which was released in the mid-1990s and became an industry standard just as the Internet arrived, helped the company become a market leader by the late 1990s. However, the dot-com bubble burst, wiping off many of its clients and altering how businesses satisfy their technological demands. Sun spent the previous decade reducing and retrenching as PCs got more powerful and fewer major clients needed Sun's expensive servers. Oracle purchased Sun earlier this year, when the company's market value was a fraction of what it had previously been.

In the 1980s and 1990s, this retailer succeeded because its notion of specialty megastores coincided with a spike in American consumerism. As it expanded nationwide, Toys "R" Us pushed out numerous competitors while absorbing others. Then the tables turned, with discounters like Wal-Mart and Target, internet sites like Amazon, and smaller shops with greater quality and service dethroning the once-mighty toy behemoth. Since 2004, when private investors purchased the firm, Toys "R" Us has been on the mend. Store closures, layoffs, and downsizing have all been part of the rehabilitation, with the owners expecting that a public offering this year or next would help collect funds to pay off debt incurred when the company was aggressively expanding.

Yahoo! When Web search and aggregation were still new, Yahoo sought to charge for services like e-mail and file sharing, whereas upstart Google gave everything out for free. Customers rushed to Google, which soared to a dominating lead in search that it maintains today. Yahoo evolved into a massive Web site with strong sports, financial, and news coverage that earns billions in ad income, but it also dabbled with job-hunting services, video streaming, original entertainment, and other enterprises that it eventually sold or folded. Nonetheless, it's still on the lookout for a successful approach, and it's now partnered with Kmart in a sort of faded-glory holding company. Analysts believe that when stores close, a Web approach might salvage the company. Yahoo's rejection of a $45 billion purchase bid from Microsoft in 2008 now appears to be a massive blunder, since the company's market value has plummeted to around $19 billion. Carol Bartz took over as CEO in 2009 with a mission to sharpen the company's focus and increase profitability. One of her first acts was to form a cooperative with an old suitor, Microsoft, in order to boost income without the stress of an acquisition.

"Greatness is not in where we stand, but in what direction we are moving. We must sail sometimes with the wind and sometimes against it—but sail we must, and not drift, nor lie at anchor."
—Oliver Wendell Holmes

P&G was aware of toothpaste thirty years ago.Gleem whitened your teeth, while Crest protected you from cavities. P & G had more than two brands in several areas, so having two brands in one category worked. They introduced a new brand if they intended to cover a variety of customer benefits. However, marketing expenditures skyrocketed, making it easier for major retailers like Walmart—who were now in charge—to promote mega-brands. As a result, Gleem was dubbed "Crest Whitening." Mega-brands reigned supreme throughout the 1990s and early 2000s. Niche companies lacked the scalability to make it onto the shelves of large supermarkets. That didn't imply that shoppers didn't desire niche brands; it just meant they couldn't find them. But only for a short time. Both P & G and Nestle had a scattering of mavericks in the 1980s. People would swarm around them, eager to take advantage of their vigor. Others, though, sought to force them out because they refused to conform. Mavericks must be safeguarded. This is something that wise leaders are aware of. They are not treated well by today's evaluation systems, which rely on success on adhering to a set of standardized norms. Mavericks all across the world started to go the way of the woolly mammoth as the millennium arrived. In the last two decades, neither P&G nor Nestle have produced a breakthrough invention. Their CEOs are bright and inspiring, but a business without mavericks is like a stew without spices. It doesn't matter how wonderful the meat is if it's not seasoned and served with a sauce. Despite the fact that everyone understands that the only constant in the world is change, individuals resist change for a variety of reasons, including fear of failure, criticism, and the unknown. They frequently believe that the devil they know is superior to an unknown angel. They accept the status quo and eventually go extinct. Alternatively, they may fail to adapt to new times and technology, resulting in the same destiny.

Today's Business- companies that are able to find a balance between the expectations of the organization and the requirements of their employees emerge as winning employer brands. The way we work has to be one of the most significant parts of human life that has irreversibly changed since the COVID-19 epidemic. While companies and employees initially struggled with the work-from-home challenge, they eventually came to terms with it without sacrificing productivity. Now that the pandemic has subsided, companies and employees are realizing that the future of work will most likely be a hybrid, a judicious mix of working from the office and working from anywhere, whenever needed. This must be a balance that benefits both sides—organizations must ensure they are receiving the most productive output from their personnel, and individuals must know that their employers can provide them with the freedom to work from anywhere whenever they need it. A preferred employer brand, on the other hand, is much more than simply providing its employees with workplace flexibility. The cloud holds the key to success. Amazon created "Amazon Web Services" (Cloud) to help businesses avoid the high cost of infrastructure. AWS has become a valuable business generator. Amazon has also created a whole ecosystem of products and services that are made possible by its Prime membership, and it is the world's most profitable internet firm. Keeping a winning streak alive Tencent, a Chinese global conglomerate holding corporation created in 1998, has evolved from an online messenger and video game firm to a technology company with interests in entertainment, autonomous vehicles, cloud computing, and financial technology.

Microsoft is changing the way businesses are run. Microsoft, founded by Bill Gates and Paul Allen, has evolved from a company that primarily sold goods, licensing (IP), and devices to a cloud-based platform-as-a-service company. Orsted: I'm relying on the wind. This Danish power firm grew from a state-owned oil and gas exploration and production corporation to become the world's largest offshore wind farm company when it went public in 2016. Supporting SMEs with Intuit Intuit has evolved from a product and service supplier to an online financial services ecosystem for small and medium-sized businesses (SMEs). TurboTax is a consumer tax preparation application. QuickBooks, a small company accounting package, ProConnect Tax Online, ProSeries, and Lacerte, and several payroll programs are all produced by Intuit.

Moving beyond insurance for Ping An Ping An, a Chinese holding conglomerate, was founded as a financial services and insurance firm. Its divisions mostly deal with insurance, banking, and financial services. The company evolved into a cloud tech company that specializes in finance and AI-based medical imaging and diagnostics. DBS Bank is a Singapore-based international banking and financial services organization. The Development Bank of Singapore Limited was the company's previous name until 2003, when it was changed to its current name. The bank evolved from a typical regional bank to a worldwide digital platform corporation based on a *"27,000-person startup"* cultural concept. It was named *"Best Bank in the World"* in 2018.

For the past 25 years, Fortune and our partner, Great Place to Work, have published the Best Companies list, with the last two being particularly tumultuous. While COVID-19 has irrevocably altered the way we work, the greatest companies are stepping up to help their workers navigate unfamiliar seas. Continue reading to learn what makes a firm stand apart. (Hint: a little more variety, flexibility, and paid time off go a long way.) long periods of inactivity. employees who felt alone and overworked. COVID was there with everything. Nonetheless, these businesses not only made it through, but also became role models. The message appears to be clear: companies that treat their employees properly during difficult times will attract talent.

Even as the fight for talent heats up, businesses that treat their employees properly in the hardest of circumstances will attract talent. The 100 hottest workplaces—and how they stay that way—are listed below. Big Tech now controls Fortune's annual survey of company reputation, just as it does our economy. For the third year in a row, Apple, Amazon, and Microsoft are ranked first, second, and third, respectively, for the third year in a row, according to our poll of 3,700 business executives, directors, and analysts. It's Apple's 15th year in a row at the top, a fitting crowning for the world's most valuable corporation. Companies on the front lines of the medical struggle received new respect as a worldwide epidemic dragged into its third year. Pfizer is one of the most effective COVID-19 co-developers. For the first time in 16 years, Pfizer, codeveloper of one of the most successful COVID-19 vaccines, jumped all the way to No. 4 on our All-Stars list. Danaher (No. 37) made its top 50 debut, with COVID diagnostics and drug-development equipment being critical in the fight against the new coronavirus.

Global equity markets have made a significant comeback since the COVID-19 disaster. As of March 31, 2021, the world's top 100 corporations were valued at a record-breaking $31.7 trillion, up 48 percent year over year. In comparison, the combined GDP of the United States and China in 2020 was $35.7 trillion. We used PwC data to create today's picture, which shows the world's largest enterprises by market value, as well as the nations and industries from which they come.

Tesla's market value increased by 565 percent, making Elon Musk the world's richest person for the time being. Meituan, a food delivery platform, and PayPal, a payment processing company, both saw their market capitalizations rise by 221 percent and 151 percent, respectively, as e-commerce popularity grew. Swiss firms Nestlé, Novartis, and Roche Holding, on the other hand, were all among the worst ten companies in terms of market capitalization growth. With a -12 percent drop, China Mobile was the only business to lose ground. The firm was delisted from the New York

Stock Exchange.

A good organization is one where people want to come to work every Monday morning, one that clearly defines its purpose, core values, and mission for its employees, and one that fosters an inclusive, enabling environment in which they can achieve their full potential both personally and professionally. Employees consider Amazon to be India's best employer because of the clarity of the company's aims, growth prospects, and work flexibility. According to a study done by Business Today, Amazon India is the best company to work for in India. The poll highlighted areas of Amazon's work culture that were strong in the fabric, such as development and learning opportunities, clarity of business goals, and work flexibility.

The India Today Group's Business Today conducts an annual study to determine the top 25 best companies to work for in India. It included topics such as staff growth initiatives, well-being, engagement, and thinking beyond the box. Other firms in the top ten are Google India, Tata Consultancy Services, Accenture, Microsoft, DHL Express, Adobe India, HDFC, Pfizer Ltd., and Tata Steel. Employees at Amazon India have embraced the Day 1 culture, with each person contributing to making each day a better day for their coworkers and consumers.

A pleasant workplace can be your cutting-edge advantage because it creates a positive work culture. Your attitude and manner are reflected on your team. Bliss is a virtue that should be flaunted. Your aura in the workplace has a direct impact on your people as a leader. As a result, when you show pleasure and optimism, you're teaching your employees to do the same. Always attempt to convey gratitude and appreciation for the work of your teammates. Complimenting little accomplishments and praising colleagues in meetings or in an appreciation note may have a significant impact on their morale. Their happiness is truly linked to the awareness that their labor adds value to the company. It is your responsibility as a leader to instill a feeling of purpose in your colleagues' work. This will give them a sense of purpose, motivating them to strive even harder. An engaged crew is more productive and willing to go above and beyond to help your company flourish. This has a deeper meaning than merely proximity. It takes a team to be successful. If you can't keep your staff pleased, you won't be successful. Speak with them. Learn about their objectives, aspirations, and motivators. When you consider your team as your family first, rather than merely a group of individuals working for you, a positive work culture emerges on its own. It takes more than simply being a leader to be a good leader. It's also about forming a fantastic team and creating a positive work atmosphere. If your staff look forward to coming to work every day, you've accomplished a significant aim. Fostering happy workers is the first step in creating a great corporate culture.

What factors contribute to the strength of a company's culture? It's no surprise that many businesses struggle to develop a distinctive and appealing workplace culture. Organizational culture, defined as the shared values, attitudes, and stories that guide individuals inside a company, may be difficult to define and develop, not to mention time-consuming. One thing is certain: a positive company culture attracts top talent. It has the potential to provide you access to the greatest talent in your business and serve as the glue that keeps your best workers on board. Indeed, 49% of workers would quit their current positions for a lower-paying position at a company with a superior culture. So, how can you make your culture one of your most valuable assets?

Adobe, the multimedia and creativity software behemoth, has earned a reputation for valuing quality, innovation, and opportunity in all it does. Indeed's top-rated workplace of 2019 was them, and they've been on Adobe fosters a healthy business culture by providing employees with highly competitive perks such as up to 16 weeks of paid maternity leave, paid time off, and retirement benefits. Adobe also has two company-wide breaks each year, one in the summer and one in the winter, during which all employees must relax and recharge.Aside from perks, the organization strives to foster a culture of diversity, inclusiveness, and justice in the workplace. Adobe thinks that individuals are more imaginative and effective when they feel valued and included. They urge their workers to value each other's differences, to assist one another to be heard, to think about what people can offer to the table, to rethink daily routines, and to stand out for what they require. Adobe has made a strong commitment to equality and has spent a significant amount of time and effort promoting pay and opportunity equity across the company.Adobe does this by ensuring that employees in similar positions and locations are compensated equitably, as well as by looking to determine if promotions and lateral career movements are occurring across demographic groupings. Adobe aspires to foster a culture that values and honors all workers' efforts.

Southwest Airlines began operations in 1971 with only three planes and has since expanded to employ over 60,000 people. One of its most prized assets is its culture. Herb Kelleher, the company's founder, is credited with establishing the belief that happy workers lead to happy customers, and profit follows. Appreciation, acknowledgement, and celebration are key to Southwest's service culture. Employees at Southwest take the opportunity to acknowledge one another in official and informal ways, such as through internal awards and activities.

"Our values—authentic, inventive, involved, and extraordinary—are founded on the belief that our people and how we treat one another are what make us a great business, Valuing the diverse life experiences that each person brings to work every day is what diversity is all about. It is essential to our success. **"stated Shantanu Narayen, Chairman, President, and CEO of Adobe.**

Considering applicants that will contribute new, fresh, and unusual ideas to your team—*"adding"* something that wasn't there before—is what hiring for culture add entails. You can establish an organization of individuals that brings varied abilities, experiences, and views to the table by recruiting for cultural fit, which leads to greater creativity and a stronger, better-performing firm.

Employees who feel involved and informed about critical events and choices are more engaged and driven to perform at their best.

In fact, according to a new Harvard Business Review Analytic Services analysis on workplace well-being, openness and transparency from top executives help to foster confidence among employees. Being transparent and vulnerable also contributes to the development of a trusting culture.And one of the most significant factors in a successful workplace culture that attracts and retains people is trust.

Considering applicants that will contribute new, fresh, and unusual ideas to your team—"adding" something that wasn't there before—is what hiring for culture add entails. You can establish an organization of individuals that brings varied abilities, experiences, and views to the table by recruiting for cultural fit, which leads to greater creativity and a stronger, better-performing firm. Employees who feel involved and informed about critical events and choices are more engaged and driven to perform at their best. In fact, according to a new Harvard Business Review Analytic Services analysis on workplace well-being, openness and transparency from top executives help to foster confidence among employees. Being transparent and vulnerable also contributes to the development of a trusting culture.And one of the most significant factors in a successful workplace culture that attracts and retains people is trust. Make people feel as if they are a part of something important. While attempts to promote diversity and inclusion are beneficial, belonging goes a step farther. Employees' feelings of safety and belonging may promote communication, cooperation, and alignment, which can lead to increased income. It's not always easy to create a sense of belonging. You may assess and gauge your efforts using employee engagement surveys, in addition to encouraging your employees to be themselves, follow their instincts, and become involved with the rest of their tribe on a daily basis.Make sure to build your office with a sense of belonging in mind, such as a common area where employees may congregate. Finally, allowing employees to contact one another on a regular basis will assist in building a sense of belonging. Finally, demonstrating that you care about your staff will encourage them to stay with you. Paying employees fairly, demonstrating that you care about their careers, and supporting good work practices, such as avoiding overworking, are just a few examples. These organizational culture examples demonstrate that organizations that have a strong organizational culture are more effective at both keeping skilled employees and recruiting new prospects.These organizations aren't the only ones with successful organizational cultures. Any firm, large or small, may enhance its workplace culture by recruiting for cultural fit, promoting transparency, cultivating a sense of belonging, and demonstrating appreciation for their workers.

To cultivate a high-performing workforce and engage your people, you must change the methods by which you drive performance and build trust. The change away from annual ratings and toward regular check-ins is a fantastic start toward what's known as performance engagement. With fewer forms, no ratings, and no invasive supervision, we were able to streamline our procedures. We spent a lot of time teaching our executives how to get the most out of these tools. A candidate experience plan should be a top focus as part of the established culture. You may get a lot of information concerning your candidate's experience on the internet. If your applicant experience is terrible, it has a significant influence on the entire brand of your firm. Take a few minutes to look up your company's web reviews and ratings if you haven't already. More than 80% of candidates looked at Glassdoor.com before interviewing, according to an internal poll we conducted at Panasonic, so you should be aware of what's being said about your company on social media.

What should you do if you are dissatisfied with your rating? Take action based on what you've learned from the comments you've received online. For example, to guarantee that we communicated with applicants effectively, we modified the way we talked with them drastically. For example, we transformed our interview procedures into high-touch, VIP experiences by drastically altering how we interacted with candidates to guarantee we kept in touch with them throughout the whole interview process. This does not imply that you should resort to high-priced hotels and limos, but rather that you should engage in extensive contact, follow-up, and feedback. It ensures that people who aren't chosen for a job are treated equally to those who are. Complete surveys before, during, and after the process to see what other holes in your procedures need to be addressed.

Panasonic also believes that a commitment to inclusion and diversity is critical to building a place where people want to work. We can actually affect a corporate culture by using the numerous voices of employees with diverse backgrounds, views, and experiences. Invest time in developing recruiting techniques and creating internal community groups as part of your diversity and inclusion plan. Invest effort in developing recruitment methods, internal community groups, and a diversity leadership program as part of your diversity and inclusion plan to not just recruit for the gaps you have, but also to retain top, diverse talent after you employ them.

You've probably noticed that I didn't mention free coffee, massage chairs, happy hour, fitness centers, amazing perks, development/training, or competitive salary. All of these things have their place, and workers appreciate them, but when we asked our employees what kept them coming back to work each day, these items were not among the top answers. Having a fantastic culture, their personal experiences working with their supervisors, how we engage them as a leadership team to enhance their performance, and the diversity and inclusion programs we have in place were all high on the list.

Don't merely aim to be a fantastic place to work; commit to putting in the effort and attention required to make it happen. Concentrate on identifying the company's ideal culture before beginning to live it. Simplify the performance engagement process and make it more focused on developing connections between managers and workers so that deep and meaningful conversations can take place. Take action on any negative comments you may have received about your recruitment and interviewing processes in order to enhance the applicant experience and employer brand. Develop diversity and inclusion initiatives that attract people with diverse backgrounds, perspectives, and experiences to your company. Make your workplace a place where people come to work because they want to, not because they have to.

Being good isn't enough for companies. Excellence must be the objective of those who wish to be the market's top and timeless option. Organizational greatness is attained through emphasis on culture and strategy. The Evidence-Based Leadership Framework and the Nine Principles for Organizational Excellence work together to foster a high-performing workplace culture and to provide ways of achieving outstanding results.

The Evidence-Based Leadership Framework is guided by the Nine Principles for Organizational Excellence. When followed to the letter, these principles provide businesses with a roadmap for building a culture of excellence. Set high expectations in order to achieve the desired results while remaining true to your goals and beliefs. Track progress on a continuous basis to obtain results while maintaining an improvement mentality.With much care and attention, serve others. People may be coached to perform at their best at work. In the workplace, pay attention to aspirations and desires. Commit to individual accountability in order to attain corporate objectives. To move the organization in the right direction, use consistent methods. People understand why what they do is important. Recognize and reward those who collaborate to achieve results. To what extent have you established appropriate goals with appropriate accountability and leadership development? Do you have a structure and methods in place for managing individual performance, such as recognizing strong work and delivering critical feedback on areas of weakness?

Are executives constantly implementing strategies, procedures, and tools across the organization? What are you up to, and where do you want to go? What are your procedures for disseminating important results and seeking feedback for improvement? Do you have service excellence standards, and do your staff know what they are? How much do you invest in staff development at all levels? How can you tell if your staff are engaged? What do you expect of each employee to ensure the organization's success? Do employee goals align with the top priority for collective success? Do workers understand the organization's and individuals' goals, as well as how they are expected to contribute? How effectively do you recognise what works so that others may see what is right?

Organizational excellence is a concept used frequently by businesses to express how they attempt to differentiate themselves from one another by putting systems in place to inspire people to better serve consumers. However, there is no pattern for how to carry it out, and firms, while recognising the need for organizational excellence, have varied approaches to accomplishing it. When it comes to organizational excellence, it is not one system or technique that is superior to another, but rather all systems, operations, organisations, and people must be able to function in unison. To attain organizational excellence, each person must have the critical qualifications to do a task well and be motivated.

Companies can improve organizational excellence among their employees by designing appropriate training for them, and in order to motivate them, employees must believe that there are clearly defined and transparent processes that determine who gets a pay raise, who gets promoted, and who gets training opportunities. Managers must establish explicit, quantifiable, achievable, reasonable, and time-bound performance objectives for each employee. Companies that give competent personnel authority over their activities allow them to fully utilise their abilities, provide input on process changes, and acquire new skills.

Summing Up

Many of the world's top corporations have failed, downsized, become outdated or been purchased by stronger competitors since 1985. The first stage is to define and articulate your competitive advantage, then compare it to those of your competitors. Differentiating your company from the competition might be done through marketable features or cheap operating costs. Most of these companies are still viable rivals that might one day innovate their way back to glory. The leadership imperative of the twenty-first century may be strategic change. To be relevant and profitable, you must find and preserve your competitive advantages by consistently analyzing the market and upgrading your products and services. Focus on building circumstances for collaborative leadership and participation among workers and consumers. Maintaining a competitive edge will be easier with a continuous improvement program. A pleasant workplace can be your cutting-edge advantage because it creates a positive work culture. Your aura in the workplace has a direct impact on your people as a leader. An engaged crew is more productive and willing to go above and beyond to help your company flourish. A positive company culture attracts top talent.That is what hiring for culture fit entails. One of the most significant factors in a successful workplace culture that attracts and retains people is trust. Being transparent and vulnerable also contributes to the development of a trusting culture. Finally, allowing employees to contact one another on a regular basis will assist in building a sense of belonging.

CHAPTER EIGHT

LEADERSHIP CAPABILITIES

Leadership Is At The Heart Of Organizational Excellence

"The pessimist complains about the wind. The optimist expects it to change. The leader adjusts the sails."

-John Maxwell

Great leaders are ordinary individuals who possess specific characteristics that distinguish them from others and enable them to accomplish amazing results. Regardless of cultural, gender, or age disparities, all leaders who have been true inspirations to their teams exhibit similar patterns of behavior. Assume you want to create the finest firm to work for on the planet. What would it be like if you could? For the past three years, you've been ideal organization in surveys and seminars throughout the world. Study on the relationship between authenticity and effective leadership led to this purpose. Simply put, people will not follow a leader who appears to be untrustworthy. However, the executives we spoke with insisted that in order to be honest, they needed to work for an authentic company.Having strong personal and organizational values, being modest, ethical in all things, treating everyone equally, and remaining collected, calm, and empathic. A visionary sees a future that inspires others, is passionate about it, strategic about it, and is laser-focused on it. Leaders define their minimal standards of excellence and then go out to demonstrate to others how to achieve them. Teams that collaborate effectively produce amazing results.

Businesses with almost equal possibilities throughout the critical years — bought into the above-mentioned change myths and failed to make the transition from excellent to outstanding. It's a terrible idea to determine where to drive the bus before you've gotten the appropriate people on board and the wrong people off. You won't have to worry about inspiring your passengers if you have the appropriate individuals on board. The appropriate individuals are self-motivated. There's nothing like being part of a team that is expected to provide outstanding outcomes. Nothing else matters if you have the wrong individuals on the bus. Even if you're on the correct track, you won't be able to accomplish greatness. With average personnel and a great vision, you'll get mediocre outcomes. Leaders build trust and develop teams by assisting each member in working in a transparent and accountable manner. Any successful business should be built on the foundation of honesty and sincerity. Two creatures are shown in this drawing: a fox and a hedgehog. Which of the two are you? According to an old Greek tale, hedgehogs know one large thing, but foxes know many minor things. It turns out that all good-to-great leaders are hedgehogs. They understand how to reduce a complicated world to a single organizing principle—the type of fundamental concept that unites, organizes, and leads all decisions. That isn't to argue that hedgehogs are simple creatures. Leaders of good-to-great firms build hedgehogs. A concept that is basic yet represents piercing insight and deep understanding, similar to great thinkers who take complexity and reduce it down into simple, yet profound, concepts (Adam Smith and the invisible hand, Darwin and evolution).

It's not a secret. Leaders who are effective generate successful organizations. How? These business executives have a set of good traits that distinguish them from their organizations. We also know that ineffective leaders contribute to dysfunctional companies. What are the beneficial qualities of a successful corporate leader? What about the top seven? Various business journals investigate and report on these top attributes of successful leaders on a regular basis. The list that emerges is consistent and demonstrates the talents and actions of the most effective leaders. Forbes, Fortune, Inc., and Entrepreneur are among these periodicals. The most often mentioned traits Here are some of the most important characteristics of effective leaders in many sectors and companies of various sizes: In all settings and contexts, integrity means being honest, truthful, trustworthy, consistent, transparent, responsible, and accountable. Speaking, writing, and (particularly) listening are all ways to create an open two-way information exchange with workers, customers, and others. Positive, brave, fearless, and optimistic, with a preference for decisive action and outcomes. Staying self-aware, courteous of others, intuitive, instinctive, anticipatory, and aware of the work environment are all examples of mindfulness. Initiator: inventing new streams of people, goods, services, processes, markets, and activities to ensure the company's long-term prosperity. Supportive behavior includes being trustworthy, establishing trust, delegating, being responsive, focused, and engaged, as well as cooperating and collaborating. Being principled means having strong personal and organizational values, being modest, and acting ethically in all situations.

Leaders may influence their workplace to reflect ethical behavior as a key value by providing an example.They lay down guidelines for people to follow as well as goals that they should strive for. Inspirational leaders are enthused by the prospect of the future and encourage their teams to share their vision of what the company may become. The best leaders, in particular, are excellent team builders. They interact and connect with others, are natural networkers, are active in recognizing and rewarding great work, are persuasive, and have a strong understanding of their objectives.Legacy leaders, above all, are genuine. Authenticity attracts and motivates those who share your values. When we think, say, and act from our heart and soul—our actual inner self—we are being authentic. Being real in business takes guts because we become vulnerable when we allow our often-protected inner self to be seen. The benefits of established soul-to-soul and heart-to-heart ties, on the other hand, can be substantial.

Authenticity validates my identity. Others are aware of the situation.Southwest Airlines‘ Herb Keller, Amazon's Jeff Bezos, Starbucks' Howard Schultz, Apple's Steve Jobs (and his successor Tim Cook), and Walmart's Sam Walton are just a few examples of brilliant leaders who embodied these talents. Henry Ford, Thomas Edison, and George Eastman (Kodak), according to history, were excellent commercial executives. And there are plenty more. What does it take for your firm to come up with a hedgehog concept? Begin by addressing the harsh realities. During the transition from excellent to outstanding, the management atmosphere resembles a raging scientific discussion, with clever, tough-minded individuals scrutinizing hard data and disputing what those findings imply. The goal isn't to win the discussion, but to come up with the greatest solutions and, in the end, to settle on a viable hedgehog concept. Kimberly-Clark emerged as the world's leading paper-based consumer-products firm, topping P & G in six of eight categories and outright controlling its longtime archrival, Scott Paper. Kimberly-Clark outperformed the market by four times under Darwin Smith, comfortably outperforming such renowned firms as Coca-Cola, General Electric, Hewlett-Packard, and 3M. Take a peek at your workstation. If you're like most hard-charging bosses, you have a well-articulated to-do list. Take a look at this: What's on your list of things to quit doing? We've all heard that leaders are the ones who make things happen, and it's true: it takes a lot of work to push that flywheel. But it's also true that good-to-great leaders stand out for their unwavering determination to quit doing anything that doesn't fit neatly into their Hedgehog Concept. Darwin Smith and his management team faced a challenge when developing the Hedgehog Concept for Kimberly-Clark. On the one hand, they saw that the greatest way to greatness was through the consumer industry, where the corporation had established world-class capacity in the development of the Kleenex brand.

"I think the combination of graduate education in a field like Computer Science and the opportunity to apply this in a work environment like Microsoft is what drove me. The impact these

opportunities create can lead to work that has a broad, worldwide impact" – Satya Nadella

Leaders open up tremendous opportunities for everyone if they work together as a team. Great leaders question the status quo and search for methods to achieve the same thing in a more efficient manner. They are willing to try new things, are not afraid of taking risks, and see failures as opportunities to learn. Jim Collins and his colleagues were led to crucial themes by a number of unanticipated discrepancies when evaluating and coding the many aspects of the good-to-great organizations and their comparisons. Bringing in high-profile, celebrity CEOs to whip a firm into shape actually hurts a company's capacity to go from excellent to outstanding. *"Strategy,"* defined as the creation of a long-term plan of any type, has no link to good-to-great performance. Long-term plans were in place for both the good-to-great and comparative firms. When it came to making the move from excellent to outstanding, technology was unimportant. It aids in the acceleration of a transition, but it is not essential for it to begin.

In my experience, successful people shoot for the stars, put their hearts on the line in every battle, and ultimately discover that the lessons learned from the pursuit of excellence mean much more than the immediate trophies and glory. - Josh Waitzkin

A good leader is aware of each of his team members' talents and flaws. He may free up time to focus on higher-level activities by distributing jobs correctly and trusting the team with his ideas. Recognizing individual contributions and celebrating triumphs works wonders, and leaders that do so motivate their employees to work twice as hard! Genuine gratitude fuels perseverance and encourages teams to work with authenticity. A lack of authenticity leads to inconsistency, which is typically manifested as a failure to apply solutions evenly. Over time, this leads to genuine inequity and also creates a strong perception of a lack of workplace justice. Is it unfair or illegal? Repeated inconsistency in dealing with conflict (e.g., ignoring misconduct, conducting sham investigations into claims of misconduct, uneven distribution of consequences when misconduct is proven) not only erodes trust, but also increases the likelihood that any level of misconduct will be perceived as not only unfair, but also illegal. This raises the likelihood that they may file internal or external legal claims. If the mistake is made internally, the employer must follow the rules and undertake a formal workplace inquiry. Alternatively, the employee might file a lawsuit. There is also another option in today's social media–fueled environment. A grievance filed by an employee might end up on a blog, an employer review website, a social networking site, or as a front-page exposé in a major newspaper. An employment lawsuit could have been yesterday's top workplace dread. Today, brand value may be destroyed with the single click of a button... a button that says *"publish."*

"The single biggest way to impact an organization is to focus on leadership development. There is almost no limit to the potential of an organization that recruits good people, raises them up as leaders and continually develops them."

-John Maxwell

Every company starts with a vision, a concept that drives the company forward. This finally spreads out and gives an organization an appropriate structure. It's the equivalent of starting a family. Some people fail, while others live happily ever after. You won't be able to achieve the results you want until you have an employee-centric culture that prioritizes their well-being. The bottom line is that you want to keep your staff happy and give them positive experiences.

Organizational excellence encompasses the whole spectrum of corporate management and the way the entire business is conducted, with the goal of achieving world-class status. Your employees apply your leadership principles to guide their work, which defines your work culture. Strive to be Earth's Best Employer is one of them. It is a value that urges leaders to lead with empathy, enjoy themselves at work, and make it simple for others to enjoy themselves. The other is that success and scale bring with them a great deal of responsibility. This album challenges leaders to be modest and careful about the consequences of their actions (especially the unintended consequences), as well as to be accountable to their local communities, the environment, and future generations.

A leader is someone who uses threats or authority to exert influence on subordinates and others solely for the good or welfare of the community or groups that chose or elected him/her as their leader. It is not useless to state that a leader is someone who motivates others and encourages them to obey him or her willingly rather than under duress. A leader is a person who represents his community's or group's desires and needs and whose activities are solely for the welfare and benefit of that group. There are two general types of leaders: formal and informal. Under the pretext of a specific rank or position, a leader who has been designated as such and has been granted certain authorities to carry out the duty. A formal leader is not a natural leader since they are chosen or elected in a bureaucratic organization through a procedure for a specific period of time, with specific powers delegated to the extent that organizational goals and objectives are met. Leaders are the heroes and assets of the organizations or communities to which they belong, and they have the basic goal of completing the task set before them with the help of their groups with confidence. It is one of the leader's duties and responsibilities to properly communicate the task to the group and muster up their courage in all the ways required, to take suggestions from the group members to evaluate the group members' attitude, and to coordinate the efforts of the group members. A leader must possess the following abilities in order to achieve organizational goals and objectives and increase his group's efficiency.Leadership is the ability of an organization to build strength in the form of manpower confidence and high morale, both of which lead to the organization's profitability. This is only achievable when the organization's leaders or leadership stay educated about the demands of the organization. A task is a test of an organization's capacity to function in any environment, such as a critical and tough period, by making the best and most beneficial decisions possible. Coordination between leadership and manpower is a critical component for an organization's success and completion of difficult tasks. Too many leaders have no idea what they don't know and have no desire to learn. Blind spots, on the other hand, can emerge in predictable ways and can be addressed. Much like driving a car, you can't be effective if there are vast, dangerous blind zones all around you. Approximately half of the employees promoted to C-level leadership roles inside a firm perform below expectations. Your cross-functional team will emerge from Leadership for Organizational Excellence cohesive, collaborative, and focused on a single goal. They'll make organizational breakthroughs in strategy, procedure, and execution. As a result of the uncertainty, an us-versus-them mindset emerges, causing even more division and mistrust. Increased division leads to a decline in empathy and self-awareness. It becomes practically hard to perceive the situation from the other person's point of view, as well as to be self-aware and modest enough to confess errors. When acts are viewed through this lens of mistrust and secrecy, they are more likely to be taken negatively, resulting in drama. The us-versus-them mentality becomes permissive, and bad behavior is tolerated. And tolerance invariably breeds more heinous actions since the bad actor is emboldened by the tolerance. After all, in our society, problems are always attributed to the person on the other side. As a result, you fail to see circumstances objectively and instead see them through the prism of expedient blame. You cloak yourselves under the guise of *"business choices."*

The absence of transparency is a classic example. Companies construct shrouds of secrecy because they believe they are forbidden from discussing *"confidential," "private," or "personal"* information. In certain cases, the information on why someone was reprimanded or penalized is inaccurate or incomplete. In others, it's implementing large-scale corporate changes (reorganizations, leadership changes, and so on) behind an impenetrable wall, with no employee involvement or knowledge. Regardless of the specific secret, two lessons stand out: Employees know more than you believe they do trying to deceive them is clear to them, and you end up doing more harm than good since they realize you're lying employees. It truly does pay to be honest, as old-fashioned as it may sound. Confusing unjust and unlawful behavior, an unequal playing field (or the reasonable sense of one), and secrecy do not go together nicely. This sends one of two messages to employees. The first is this: don't come to me with a complaint unless it's about illegal behavior. Employers don't find out about difficulties until they've reached a crisis point when this happens. The second lesson is that when you do raise your issues, use charged legal rhetoric like *"hostile work environment"* and *"retaliation"* instead of stating facts and consequences.

As a result, rather than solving problems, the firm leader goes into defense mode. This merry-go-round of posturing demonstrates the need to establish a shared and effective business vocabulary—one that genuinely aims to solve the workplace drama problem. As one side believes the other is out to get them, blind spots form, and our capacity to predict and respond to drama deteriorates. Of course, shifting someone to a lesser position on the organizational chart during a reorganization may cause resentment and accusations of injustice, but reorganization strategists believe, *"Hey, they're lucky to have a job."*

The capacity to foresee and plan for drama is a crucial talent that, sadly, most businesses lack. Clearly, the solution is to start recruiting everyone who ticks the *"diversity box"* regardless of qualifications. While this may address your short-term financial problem, it will surely build animosity, harm your business, and do little to assist with *"diversity statistics"* in the long run because you are putting the prospects up to fail. You execute ineffective solutions or overcorrect because we don't recognize the fundamental reasons for the drama. In either scenario, we exacerbate an already difficult situation. In today's workplace, the most common response to workplace drama is to "examine our policies and procedures." There are more rules. HR and leadership are increasingly seen as police, exacerbating the drama rather than alleviating it. Overcorrection is just as harmful as applying the incorrect solution. This, too, stems from a failure to consider what may truly fix the problem, critically and creatively. Your company's diversity indicators reflect a low number of underrepresented employees. Clearly, the solution is to start recruiting everyone who ticks the *"diversity box"* regardless of their qualifications.

For many people in corporate world , the idea of apologizing is unthinkable. It is, nevertheless, a necessary component if you are to shift the needle on culture. You all make errors. You are incapable of anticipating issues. You don't give ourselves enough time to make sound judgments. You disregard issues in the hope that they will go away. Making a mistake is human; neglecting to acknowledge and rectify the situation is catastrophic. Inauthentic companies are made up of CEOs that refuse to confess wrongdoing, prolonging the cycle of mistrust. These triggers, if left unchecked, produce a poor work atmosphere and have concrete (and negative) consequences. Widespread distrust results in low morale and productivity, as well as significant (and unneeded) turnover, increasing allegations of injustice, difficulty recruiting and maintaining top people, legal claims, and, of course, brand harm.

The leadership and the rest of the organization disagree on fundamental issues. Employees are not as enthusiastic about new corporate initiatives as they once were.The workplace has become toxic; morale is low, new hires feel isolated, employees are unconcerned about results, and your best employees have gone silent. Yes, it's time to make a shift. But what precisely is it? What do you do first? Business strategy is influenced by cultural factors. Deloitte's global culture model identifies eight categories in which executives must make deliberate choices and judgments in order to realign culture with business objectives. There are several specific places where disruption must occur in order for organizational culture to change course in the middle of the game. Leaders must clearly define the goal and integrate it into all company efforts. On its part, "People Practises" must accept it comprehensively in text and spirit. The business and operational procedures must keep up with the pace. Every stage of the trip requires infrastructure and systems to support it. And, at any given time, all thinking and activity must be mapped forward to the overarching goal of the organizational journey. In the video below, Deloitte uses a five-lever method to maximize cultural re-engineering.

To sum up, leadership plays a critical role in the advancement of companies. Only co-ordination and confidence across concerns and groups of concerns can produce effective and meaningful work, and only the function of leadership can achieve this co-ordination and confidence, since business concerns cannot meet the needs of every single employee or member of the workforce. As a result, by working together, the organization can achieve its goals and the groups may achieve their own goals that are aligned with the organization's.

Summing Up

Some of the most effective corporate leaders have a set of good traits that distinguish them from their organizations. Authenticity attracts and motivates those who share your values. Being real in business takes guts because we become vulnerable when we allow our inner self to be seen. Good-to-great leaders stand out for their unwavering determination to quit doing anything that doesn't fit neatly into their Hedgehog Concept.Great leaders question the status quo and search for methods to achieve the same thing in a more efficient manner.Organizational excellence encompasses the whole spectrum of corporate management and the way the entire business is conducted, with the goal of achieving world-class status. Leadership for organizational excellence is the ability of an organization to build strength in the form of manpower, confidence, and high morale. Too many leaders have no idea what they don't know and have no desire to learn. Blind spots, on the other hand, can emerge in predictable ways and can be addressed. Leaders must clearly define the goal and integrate it into all company efforts. People who *"practice"* must accept it comprehensively in text and spirit. Every stage of the trip requires infrastructure and systems to support it. The leadership and the rest of the organization disagree on fundamental issues.

CHAPTER NINE

TRUSTING ENVIRONMENT

Excellent Organizations Are Relationship-Driven And Socially Connected

"Trust is like the air we breathe – when it's present, nobody really notices; when it's absent, everybody notices." -Warren Buffett

The foundation of any business is trust. It is the foundation of any human relationship: engagement, communication, initiative, professional effort, and even any strategic objective you must complete. Social groups cannot function properly without it. Without trust, you'll end up with a broken organization with slow-moving teams. A company with a low level of trust is like a jet without gasoline. You may fumble around in it as much as you like, but it will not get you to your destination. Every initiative, job endeavor, and strategic requirement you must complete requires faith in someone. Social groups cannot function properly without it.Without trust, you'll end up with a broken organization with slow-moving teams. Because trust allows an organization to function as it should, it leads to excellent performance. It's the first line of defense against dysfunction and the first step toward improved results. Many people would not say *"trusting"* or *"trusted"* as the first word that comes to mind when asked to define their corporate culture. While we may work in pleasant locations with pleasant coworkers, the organizational culture generated by leaders is frequently viewed in a totally different light. According to the Edelman Trust Barometer 2019, trust in organizations has increased to 58% (trust in my employer for information). While this is encouraging news, there is still work to be done to unlock the productivity locked up in organizations, and leaders and managers play a key role. Let's look at how enhanced trust might help an organization using the example of flexible working. We've seen a lot of companies establish flexible working arrangements, only to have them fail miserably. The first element of this that you must address is generating meaningful dialogues that increase goal and expectation clarity, and the second is developing meaningful connections that strengthen people's trust. When these two things happen, you have a trusting workplace in which individuals may work as they see fit, producing the job that is anticipated without the need for continual *"policing."* For many leaders, the task isn't as easy as finding individuals they can trust, though that is critical. You must assist leaders and managers in changing their perceptions of what it means to be productive at work, and this is where meaningful discussions and meaningful connections come into play. Many HR departments at many companies complain that regular interactions (whether formal 1-2-1s or casual catch-ups) aren't happening frequently enough. Upskilling leaders on how to conduct these important dialogues is a common strategy used by L & D teams, but the problem that is typically overlooked is how to enable leaders and managers to recognize the importance of these talks. When workers are given a task, such as checking in with their team on a regular basis, it becomes just that—a task. Building great teams, cultivating a healthy work culture, and achieving desired outcomes all start with trust. The cost of a lack of workplace trust or a culture of trust is much higher than you may realize. According to Fast Firm, a Fortune 500 company discovered that implementing change takes an average of 89 weeks, with 39 of those weeks being a

direct result of distrust. You've probably worked in a location where people's work and emotions were unreliable, insufficient, disloyal, uncommunicative, and inconsistent.There will be occasions when you must make difficult judgments. This isn't something you should try to brush under the rug. Let them know that things might have to change and that you'll handle it professionally and compassionately. It's easy to get caught up in the trap of putting others down. For example, you might say things about them to their coworkers. If you see yourself doing this, make a mental note of it and be aware of it in the future. If you want to take it a step further, have your staff tell you when they believe you are putting them down. Sitting around reading and studying, let alone meeting up with someone over coffee, may be considered unproductive in some workplaces (outside of your break times). Going out for coffee and catching up with someone, on the other hand, may provide more value than we realize. You may be aware that spending time getting to know someone may give us a sense of assurance about them, according to Paul Zak's groundbreaking study into the neurobiology of trust. This causes oxytocin to be released, laying the groundwork for a trusting connection. Finding the "hooks" that bind us is crucial to forging lasting connections. You're all the same in some manner, whether it's our way of life, upbringing, education, or profession—we're all alike on some level.It's easy to get caught up in the trap of putting others down. For example, you might say things about them to their coworkers. If you see yourself doing this, make a mental note of it and be aware of it in the future. If you want to take it a step further, have your staff tell you when they believe you are putting them down. Assuming they haven't breached the law, you should make a point of sticking up for the team and fighting your corner. This is especially true when they are under duress. It takes guts, but it will earn you a lot of respect. It's what I call a low-trust workplace, and it can make everyone feel extremely stressed and unwelcome. People begin to take responsibility for their duties, assist one another, speak well of one another, interact more frequently, and are more productive when trust is prevalent.

People may discuss their challenges and goals in a secure environment, allowing them to attain their full potential as individuals and as a group. So, as a leader, how can you foster a culture of trust?

"You cannot prevent a major catastrophe, but you can build an organisation that is battle ready, that has high morale and has also been through a crisis, knows how to behave, trusts itself and where people trust one another. In military training, the first rule is to instill soldier with trust in their officers because without trust they won't fight." -Peter Drucker

You feel that everyone wants to be noticed, recognised, and cherished. Writing a letter to each of my direct reports is one of my favourite things to do in January. It took up the entire page and was single-spaced. After a paragraph outlining my firm's overall accomplishment, I wrote two paragraphs about each individual's contribution to that achievement. It was both a compliment and an encouragement. It was linked to actual goals they had achieved, and it included individuals I had employed and initiatives I had backed. I lit up, and then I got one the following year. Then I got one the next year.Following my own 360 review a few years later, I discovered that while I was managing up and across relatively effectively, my team felt pretty abandoned. What I believed I was providing them in terms of independence and empowerment was met with alienation and apathy. From their point of view, I had no idea what they were doing and didn't care. In a nutshell, they didn't feel noticed, recognised, or respected. I was certainly not giving these presents to my staff. As I considered methods to bridge the divide, to let them know, truly know, that I saw them, knew them, and valued their efforts, the letters my CEO penned came to mind.That was also the first year I chose to send letters to my own squad. And that was an excellent first step toward altering their minds. More than an olive branch, it was an opportunity to express in black and white the precise ways in which I saw each member of my team evolving and how much I loved them. It was a game changer for my team, and it may be a game changer for your team as well. So, by sending a lengthy personal letter, you may demonstrate to your reports that you notice, know, and respect them. Recognize that it will require time and emotional energy before you dig in.You can not just sign a Hallmark card. I type each letter, which I realise is a little impersonal, then I print it on letterhead to make it feel more professional. Furthermore, I relate particular tasks to the recipient's talents, personality, and contributions. I attempt to compose each letter in addition to all of the work I undertake for annual assessments. This allows me to evaluate everything that employee has done since the last time I wrote them a letter.It also allows me to observe each employee's year through their eyes, allowing me to support and promote the finest ways they show up for work.Finally, I incorporate personal connections, referring to non-work issues that have arisen over the years, reminding each employee that I regard them as more than simply an employee, that we may be on goal together, but we are more than our work. Finally, the letter reflects a genuine sight. I want every employee to feel known and cared for, whether they have had a difficult year or are in good standing. I'd want to thank the individual and their labour. And as a manager, the least I can do is provide that present every year. So, how about you?As you can see, creating a strong corporate culture is a continuous effort that is well worth your time. When you bring people together on a goal, develop clear leadership, build trust, and construct support mechanisms, your team becomes united on a solid cultural basis. Then you will be able to actually do big things. This course is only the beginning. If you want to go deeper, I'd be happy to recommend some other resources. To begin with, here are a few books to get you thinking about culture. In his book *"Good to Great,"* Jim Collins presents information on very successful businesses.

I'll provide the five aspects of trust in this piece so you can boost your team's morale.As a leader, you understand how critical it is to instill trust in yourself and your team. For leaders, cultivating a culture of trust is a difficult task. When you're attempting to make a change, the task becomes considerably more difficult.The way you treat individuals should not be determined by their position or influence. Good leaders understand that treating everyone equally and respectfully is an important component of building a trusting atmosphere. The great majority of individuals put in a lot of time at work and want to make a difference. People closest to the point of delivery are often the ones who perceive the most opportunities for improving working procedures or providing a far better service. Actively listen and show genuine interest. Give constructive criticism and positive comments frequently so that others understand where you're coming from and what you anticipate. You may also be transparent by owning up to your faults and being vulnerable in front of others. This demonstrates that you're not flawless, and it's a terrific approach to demonstrate that others can trust you. Your staff will learn to be more candid with you and one another if you set an example for them. Respect does not require you to agree with everyone. However, honoring their feelings fosters trust, which allows them to open up more freely. Respect is only the application of the Golden Rule: "Do unto others as you would have them do unto you." Let me offer some data on organizational trust that you should be aware of. One in three individuals do not trust their employer, according to the latest Edelman "Trust Barometer" (a poll of 33,000 people in 28 countries). They also observed that from the highest to the lowest levels, trust diminishes. For example, 64% of executives trust their companies, compared to 51% of managers and 48% of other employees.Employees stated that they trust their peers more than their company's CEO and upper-level executives. That implies that the higher you rise, the more important it becomes to establish trust with people below you. Leaders are at the forefront of building trust. Give them a task that they must complete as a group. If they fail, they will all bear the consequences. If they succeed, they will all be rewarded. A team that suffers and triumphs together stays together.

Leadership guru John C. Maxwell remarked, "People don't care how much you know until they know how much you care." When someone realizes that you regard them as a person and not simply as an employee, trust is developed. You can show people you care about them by learning more about them, expressing your appreciation to them on a regular basis, and asking for their opinions more frequently.When individuals feel appreciated, you acquire not just their trust, but also their loyalty.

"Trust is the antidote that overcomes fear – and fear is the greatest inhibitor of all to a relationship that welcomes and nurtures new ideas." -John Pepper, Disney Chairman

It has been proven that people who love their coworkers are happier and more productive—and this does not happen by chance. Providing activities focused on creating trust in teams is one approach to increase morale and create trust at the same time. When comparing a high-trust to a low-trust work environment, the leader's five TRUST components will either be present or absent. My challenge to you is to work on establishing one of the five aspects of trust every day. Today, work on being transparent; tomorrow, work on showing others respect; and so on.Continue until you've established a high-trust work atmosphere and increased workplace respect.

It's simple to claim that you trust your staff, but do you really? Do your actions demonstrate your belief that your employees will do a good job or make the best decisions? While many leaders claim to trust their employees, my experience as a consultant for complex organizations and as General Manager-Future Markets at Pierlite has taught me that their actions tell me differently. According to PwC, 55 percent of CEOs think that a lack of trust is the most serious danger to their company, yet few take steps to repair it.Trusting your staff might be intimidating; all of the "what if" situations in your head may make you want to take command. But I urge you to pause, take a breath, and consider how simply believing in your staff might enhance your business practices and performance. People who work in high-trust firms have 74 percent less stress, 50 percent higher productivity, 13 percent fewer sick days, 40 percent less burnout, and 76 percent higher engagement, according to research.It's logical. Why would you want to work for a company that didn't value your abilities, knowledge, and experience?

A lack of trust fosters emotions of powerlessness and dissatisfaction, which lead to a lack of effort and caring. According to research, 96 percent of engaged employees trust management, compared to 46 percent of disengaged employees. It's an indication of a good workplace atmosphere if you trust your colleagues and they trust you back. Collaboration and total control are just not possible for leaders. People must feel comfortable sharing their opinions and cooperating with one another in order for your business to thrive. Employees and executives attribute 86 percent of workplace failures to a lack of teamwork or open communication.

This strategy is used by Google, and they have a program known as the 20% rule. Employees at Google are expected to spend 80% of their time on duties allocated to them and 20% of their time exploring fresh and inventive ideas. Not only is Google empowering its employees by believing in their ability, but it has also resulted in some fantastic ideas like AdSense, Google News, and Gmail. While this guideline may not be available in every firm, the notion is what is important. Great things may happen if you trust your staff and have an open communication system. This will help your firm progress and flourish.

Empowerment comes from trust. Giving your staff your whole trust and believing in their ability to perform distinguishes a bunch of individuals from a team. Giving your personnel your trust does not imply that everything will go according to plan; rather, by creating a collaborative and community-focused atmosphere, your team will be able to address difficulties faster and without fear of retribution. In fact, 97 percent of employees and executives feel that a team's lack of alignment has an influence on the job or project's outcome. The foundation of a great team environment is trust.

Employees' fear of responsibility is removed when you trust your team and develop a community culture. The fear of being blamed can cause anxiety and have a negative influence on employee productivity and happiness. With 56 percent of employees reporting that anxiety at work has a negative impact on their job performance, this is an area where leaders should strive to improve. Removing the concept of individual failures and replacing them with the concept of team failures is a simple way to accomplish this. If something goes wrong, it's because of the team, so a joint solution may be developed. Problems can be discovered sooner, and solutions can be found faster, if responsibility is shifted from an individualistic logic to a team mentality. This is when trust comes into play.

Similarly, by consistently offering positive feedback that recognizes employees' accomplishments, trust and a team relationship may be developed. According to a WorkHuman Research Institute poll, 82 percent of employees who had their achievements recognized by their bosses trusted them.Recognizing employees' accomplishments not only motivates them to strive even more, but it also makes them feel connected. As a leader, you often convey your team's work to stakeholders and other employees. It's vital at this point to acknowledge everyone's work rather than take unnecessary credit. Allowing your employees to shine both inside and outside will guarantee that they remain devoted and loyal to you and the company's ultimate goals.

"Trust is the lubrication that makes it possible for organisations to work." -Warren Bennis

In all aspects of leadership, trust is essential. It's crucial to have faith in your staff if you want to have a productive and effective workplace. Employee empowerment stems from your conviction in their skills, which simplifies all aspects of your organization and allows for genuine transformation. Building reciprocal trustworthy connections is how leaders and organizations grow, from ensuring a friendly environment to looking after yourself and your health. I believe it is past time for all leaders to try to change the statistic that just one out of every three employees trusts their boss and to foster a safe and open working atmosphere.

"Those who attain any excellence commonly spend their life in one pursuit, for excellence is not often granted on easier terms." - Samuel Johnson

In her book, *"Dare to Lead,"* sociology professor Brené Brown compares trust-building to marbles in a jar. It's a fantastic analogy. When you first meet someone, you wish you could trust them. You're simply not convinced it's feasible since trust doesn't work that way. Beliefs give rise to trust. When a new member of your team enters, your assumptions about that individual are primarily speculative. They are what you anticipate or wish for. Then you fill in the blanks with what you don't know. Limited experience with someone equates to limited trust, often known as thin trust. This is the kind of trust that has shallow roots. As your relationship with someone develops, you define your values and expectations, and those roots get a bit deeper. So, how do you fill the jar with marbles or deepen the roots?

You like that your working groups have defined goals, a timetable, and deliverables. This approach enables you to mix and match working groups to facilitate professional growth and cross-pollination and ensure that knowledge is allocated where it is required. A defined timetable pushes team members to participate effectively and meet specified deadlines. You also appreciate the fact that your working groups address real-world issues and possibilities. This motivates employees and empowers them to work together to solve challenges. Concentrated work promotes the development of connections across functions and between people who rarely work side by side under normal circumstances.It also promotes common knowledge of your organization's issues and potential. Shared knowledge and time together assist in reducing the us vs. them mentality and whining that may result from compartmentalised work. So, who in your organization needs more time spent together? Perhaps this is your opportunity to assist them in developing a shared knowledge of your firm or to increase their mutual regard for one another. Creating cross-functional teams to address organizational issues or opportunities is an excellent method to foster relationships, provide professional development, and ultimately empower your team. So, what is the next challenge or opportunity that your team is eager to take on? This week, gather a group of people to form a circle. You just took on a greater responsibility at your business in managing professional development for a new generation of managers. Many of these managers were new to their positions as well as the club. They needed to spend time together in order to develop cross-functional relationships. You also need to include some professional growth. When considering solutions that could hit both targets, you choose a strategy from your higher education toolkit. You choose a book, and we read it together.Starting a book club is not a novel concept. Many businesses utilise book clubs for professional growth, to inspire innovative thinking, or to cross-pollinate employees. What is innovative is using the same book talks to speed up the process of creating trust within a team.

You'd like to provide a few ideas for building trust in your next book group. Analyze the structure first. Book clubs give a shared experience by reading the same book, and they require several points of connection to meet to discuss a chapter or two at a time as people go through the content together and consider the intersection. You worked through a basic book on entry-level management prepared by a prominent publisher for a group of newly minted managers like you.Everyone who read the book was able to relate to the content and link it to their new experiences. There was no pressure to agree with the author, and the combination of a manager learning lessons and having these real-life experiences connect resulted in a lively conversation about what was and wasn't working. When people begin talking about their experiences, someone will wade into the dangerous seas. When this happens, try to keep your enthusiasm in check because things are about to get incredibly exciting. Vulnerability led to helpful encouragement in your book club, which led to more excellent questions, and good questions led to deeper knowledge and finally shared answers.Bottom line, the group was beginning to work through its accomplishments and mistakes as a unit. Trust was gaining ground. Don't overlook the structure. Another benefit of reading the same book is that team members begin to use the author's vocabulary. Under your management, your group was building a shared style of thinking about this issue. Learning to listen properly is perhaps the most difficult aspect of managing a book group. You must ask really open-ended questions and endure terrible silence. You must encourage smaller voices to speak out and more comfortable sharers to ask more questions, but the most difficult element is listening properly, which also leads to the largest gains.

You establish trust by taking concrete actions to increase your team's social capital. You'll find a few suggestions below to get you started. To begin with, it is critical to emphasise that you must always take the first step. You're the boss. That indicates you have the authority and must make the first move. What will it resemble? That is all up to you. Consider limiting shop chatter. When it comes to appreciating individuals, it's critical to look beyond their employment. This has been quite challenging for you. You simply enjoy being there.You just enjoy being on a mission with others. So, while working around the clock makes sense for you, it does not make sense for everyone else.If you want to create trust with your team, treat them as individuals rather than as workers. Can you take a lunch break, a coffee break, a happy hour, or the first 10 minutes of your next one-on-one? Empathy is fostered via personal sharing. People see each other more clearly as they get to know one another. This, in turn, promotes care. Allow yourself to be vulnerable. Personal sharing necessitates a degree of vulnerability, which may be difficult to do. You've undoubtedly all met someone who overshares, but initiating the discussion is critical. Perhaps you could discuss an embarrassing experience or a personal failing that relates to your current situation.Others tend to follow you when you wade into the rivers of vulnerability. Building social capital will force you to include your staff in all aspects of life. Perhaps you've excelled at putting work marbles in the jar. What about your own personal marbles? If this is already your regular, that's fantastic. Is this a challenge for your team members? How can you persuade people to share personal information with you?

"Excellence is not an easy joke, if one has such an aspiration as That needs, ideas, intelligent efforts and alert mind in works..!"

Do you consider helpfulness to be something that is given or received? Which is more vulnerable, providing aid or asking for it? Requesting and getting assistance promotes vulnerability and support. It also fosters a sense of reciprocity and team buy-in. You used to think of aid almost solely as something you gave to others. You've had a rather wealthy upbringing, and you've adopted cultural beliefs that emphasise things like perseverance and self-reliance. You are frequently eager to provide assistance, but you are hesitant to seek it yourself. However, this is only half the tale.Do you consider helpfulness to be something that is given or received? Which is more vulnerable, providing aid or asking for it? Requesting and getting assistance promotes vulnerability and support. It also fosters a sense of reciprocity and team buy-in. You used to think of aid almost solely as something you gave to others. You've had a rather wealthy upbringing, and you've adopted cultural beliefs that emphasise things like perseverance and self-reliance. You are frequently eager to provide assistance, but you are hesitant to seek it yourself. However, this is only half the tale.Over the last decade, you've become more adept at asking for assistance, and learning to accept assistance has significantly altered your relationships. It may seem paradoxical, but if you want to create trust, you must ask for assistance.

Building trust is dependent on mutual support, and mutual support necessitates both parties asking for assistance. Asking for aid necessitates vulnerability, and when it comes to vulnerability, it's up to you as the leader to make the first move, right? Perhaps you have a few pointers to help you create trust by asking for assistance. First and foremost, do not submit a phoney request. This may sound obvious, but if you don't want to be vulnerable, you'll try to make a phoney request because it's going to feel safer. The issue is that fake vulnerability is unsightly. Consider asking for help where you truly need it, and then identify someone on your team who can assist you. Next, make a precise and relevant request. Being precise allows people to provide actual and meaningful support, and trust is built by asking for that meaningful aid. Finally, don't seek assistance from someone who is unable to assist you. Yes, you've seen this manoeuvre before. You want to give the impression that you're vulnerable. So you requested assistance with a really challenging situation. And the people you ask are ill-equipped to assist. This is like admitting you need help, but it's with an issue you're not intelligent enough to solve. Instead, seek assistance from those who are qualified to do so. You will receive genuine assistance. You'll also hasten the process of establishing confidence. This may appear to be a small matter, but the power of asking for aid is crucial to establishing confidence. Today is a good day to ask for aid.

You frequently take disparate pieces of information and weave them together in a way that best fits your point of view. Unfortunately, this contains your prejudices, concerns, and fears, and it seldom casts them in the best light imaginable. What would happen if you assumed your coworkers were trying their best? What if you thought somebody had good intentions even when it didn't seem like it? You feel that this is one of the keys to fostering a positive culture in your organization. When you and your team start treating each other as if everyone is acting with good intentions, you promote inquiry and understanding over blame and judgement.In practise, how does this look? You'll most likely need to develop some new behaviours. When your team has issues, they must first go directly to the source. That means no more backchannel chats, no more rant sessions, and no more gossip circles. Your team will need to be liberal with their inquiries. This is curiosity that suspends judgement in the hopes of receiving a sensible response. What if your coworker is unaware that they have insulted you? What if your manager had excellent reasons for avoiding passing on information you believed you needed? What if your report had the greatest of intentions when it inadvertently stomped on a colleague's toes, making you appear bad? However, if you add empathy to the mix, you'll be able to look at a weak argument or a bad conclusion and envisage the finest possible version of that viewpoint. You'll be able to see the choice through the eyes of the decider rather than your own.

Finally, a suggestion. You'll find yourself in circumstances when it's obvious that the individual who is irritated with you did not act with good intentions. However, even in this case, assuming positive intent will assist you in moving forward in a positive manner. This is a method that is effective even though it should not be. So, are you ready to begin? Consider a coworker who has recently irritated you and rethink the entire exchange from their point of view.Consider the finest of them. Assume your coworker tried their best and had the finest intentions. Then, jot out a few honest, non-judgmental, and forward-thinking questions to ask that colleague in order to truly grasp what happened and to open the door to feedback.The majority of employees claim that they do not receive adequate feedback. When most supervisors offer it, employees respond with argumentative defensiveness. That's why the vast majority of you shun feedback like the plague. Don't, don't, don't do it. It is vital to provide clear and timely feedback to your direct reports in order to maintain successful working relationships. It's impossible to avoid. So, how do you go about approaching it constructively? The author suggests using the 10x encouragement model. Every item of negative input should be surrounded by ten times the amount of positive feedback. When providing feedback, you must have relational equity to invest in. Now, this may require some rephrasing, so the author has a few suggestions for you. To begin with, keep in mind that your direct report is doing admirably on a variety of critical responsibilities every day. That is most likely why you looked for, hired, trained, and continue to employ that person.Reframe your perception of feedback. Every day, you must catch your staff doing something positive. And when you do, give straightforward, positive comments. Whether the feedback is favourable or negative, you propose that it be delivered in the same manner. Ask permission, provide comments, confirm understanding, and then move away.

When you arrived on time and prepared for the morning meeting, your entire team was able to work through the problem swiftly; keep doing that. When you arrived late and unprepared for your morning meeting, the whole team was put under a lot of pressure to cover for you. Can you make that right the next time? And then walk away again.Manager Tools emphasises keeping your tone and tempo consistent in each scenario. Refrain from going into too much detail. In our situation, both incidences were minor. Neither of them will require coaching. Both are simple changes that your employee may make. This type of feedback is frequent and timely. It takes the sting out of providing feedback since you've normalised it.When the majority of feedback is good, the authorization to provide it is more frequently given. It's also important to remember that feedback is about modifying behaviour, not evaluating intentions or assigning blame. You are not providing feedback if you are not attempting to assist your direct report in making improvement. Finally, remember to keep the 10X encouraging aim in mind. This was really challenging for me.Do you attempt to avoid confrontation at work, or do you put on your boxing gloves and enter the ring? As it turns out, either reaction will fail miserably. It takes courage to have difficult conversations. When you were a younger manager, your stomach could have knotted up in knots when you knew you needed to have a difficult talk. And all of that worry may be exhausting. So much so that people should attempt to avoid tough talk and make things work. I recall one season in particular when I avoided having a difficult talk with a coworker. While she and I had occasional disagreements, I believed she was working well with others and moving initiatives forward. "Why should I say anything?"I'd tell myself that. Let it go; it only affects you. Or do you really want to be the man who is now rocking the boat? " When she chose to depart, she gave herself a wake-up call. And I realised that everyone else was just trying to forget about it because I didn't seem to be having any problems. The truth is that since I didn't have the fortitude to lean in and have some difficult talks, my colleagues had to deal with the same dissatisfaction that I was. This was not only unfair to the team, but it was also unjust to the former employee. She deserved the honest dialogue that I had avoided. As Brene Brown points out in "Dare to Lead," being clear is nice.I had been cruel by avoiding the difficult talk. Finally, the employee departed. And as she did, the tension increased. Perhaps you can relate. Since then, I've realised that engaging in difficult conversations is a necessary component of sustaining successful professional relationships. And now that I've leaned in, I've learnt a lot from these discussions. If this is a problem for you, I have a few ideas for you. First and foremost, being clear is a kind thing to do. Even though it is uncomfortable, speaking truthfully is the best strategy. But, honestly, about what? Before you lean in, make sure you're clear on the behaviour you want to correct. Character assaults have no place in difficult debates.I think it's best to start there. From the outset, be straightforward, express the facts simply and concisely, invite certification, and promote other opinions. Although difficult talks might be unpleasant, they should not be dangerous. It is entirely up to you to create an environment of mutual respect and shared purpose. Taking the time to have a difficult talk may seem like a visit to the principal's office. Take the time to reframe it early on. Set a goal for the dialogue and affirm mutual respect. What are you attempting to achieve? You and the employee have a chance to join forces and work together to solve the current problem. When mutual respect is maintained, it may be a reassuring moment.Remember that every stress contains an opportunity for understanding. Consider what you could learn from the employee and this interaction. Arrive inquisitive and prepared to listen. Recognize when things are going wrong. When people don't feel comfortable in an area, they tend to become quiet or aggressive. And the sooner you detect these kinds of adjustments, the sooner you'll be able to preserve that discussion. Sometimes it's possible to reestablish safety, and other times it's necessary to take a break. In any instance, strive to preserve a sense of mutual respect while working toward a common solution. Finally, keep in mind that not having the dialogue is cruel. It's cruel to you, cruel to the team, and cruel to the situation.

Be considerate. It will be difficult at first, but it is preferable to the alternative. And, believe me, it will get easier. Work goes between the cracks when there is a lack of clarity. Work initiatives go by the wayside when there are insufficient resources and time. Great cultures promote getting work done by clarifying responsibilities and encouraging coworkers to help one another. First and foremost, it is your obligation to ensure that everyone understands which lane they are driving in. Each piece of work must be owned by someone. Even if that individual does not actually complete the service, who should I contact if the power washing has to be done? When too many people are assigned to a task, it simply does not get completed. If you are too busy or forget, nobody can help you. Nobody can expect that if you become busy or forget, someone else will just take care of things. At the same time, you want to encourage people to support one another. You mention having a one-team approach. Look, odds are that everyone on your team feels like they always have a full plate of work. If you want to ensure that all of the jobs are completed, you must ensure that your team understands who does what and that employees in your business help one another as needed.

Shared rules lead to shared expectations, and shared expectations aid in the development of trust. A healthy culture is based on clarity and trust, and ground rules help to foster both. So, if you want a healthy culture, set some ground rules for teamwork. This procedure might be short or long, depending on the team. It may just take five or ten minutes for people to discuss how they want to work together and then develop a short list of organizations with a lot of history and pretty healthy fuel. New groups take longer to form because they must go through both a relational list of things like listening and being courteous, as well as a logistical list of things like showing up on time and turning off your mobile phone. At the first meeting of our newly formed management group, the team spent some time discussing how to alternate note-taking, the use of radios and mobile phones, and how to consider the information that would remain in the room against the information that would be sent to team members. After your group has established a set of ground rules for working together, examine how you will keep those ground rules in mind. You would cease activities and return to the covenant, our ground rules, when the tension and irritation reached a boiling point. Do you adhere to these? Are they on your side? Do you want to make any changes? It takes effort to work your way through the ground rules, but it's well worth it.Returning to the ground rules also confirms expectations within your group and explains the sense of unity that groups build when they make a common commitment, even if it is a low-stakes commitment such as retreat ground rules. Finally, a word from experience. Creating a safe place, respecting all views, presuming positive intent, and questioning ideas rather than individuals are four fundamental ideas that nearly every group I've worked with has come up with in some form or another. If your team completes the ground rule exercise without addressing one of these suggestions, you may want to push them to do so.Fear, particularly fear of failure, will be one of the most difficult difficulties you'll encounter as you attempt to create a strong corporate culture. And one of the most critical processes you can create to foster an outstanding culture is how you evaluate failure. As an educator, I identify with entrepreneurial concepts such as "fail fast" and "fail forward." I've witnessed the power of failure to teach students and workers about themselves, their procedures, and the task they're attempting to do.While you may agree with my sentiment, you've probably also witnessed the blame game in your organization. Nothing stifles innovation and morale like blame, which is why Jim Collins speaks of great companies conducting autopsies without blame, and why Brene Brown replaces failures with the word learning. If you want to establish a strong corporate culture, you must examine difficulties without assigning blame. As you implement procedures to reduce blame, you will see a boost in morale and an increase in inventiveness. Here are a few things to consider when you begin. The purpose of any examination is to comprehend rather than label.The purpose of assessments in education is to determine what subject or skill the student has already mastered and then to identify areas for further improvement. Project evaluation is quite similar. Maintain your assessment's emphasis on the project itself. Work hard to understand what went wrong, much like Collins' autopsy, and remember that in every tension lies the possibility for enlightenment. As Brown proposes, considering failure as a learning opportunity raises the question, "What did we learn from this unsuccessful project?" Did we begin with the proper aim in mind? Did we allocate the appropriate resources? Has the market or the situation shifted? How do these findings inform the other initiatives we're working on now?Your team can move ahead from any setback by pausing to consider failure as a learning opportunity. When seen in this light, analysing all work creates introspective space for improving work relationships and procedures. Finally, remember that analysing without assigning blame does not imply avoiding difficult conversations or lying about how well a project went.No progress will be made until all parties involved understand what went wrong and how to improve in future opportunities.You're working hard to foster a culture in which individuals may succeed, even fail, and continue to learn and grow.Learning to analyse without assigning blame is essential for this process. Avoid the impulse to assign blame. Instead, consider failure to be a wonderful opportunity to learn, change, and progress.

I used to believe that meetings were a complete waste of time. Indeed, headlines, podcasts, and a slew of notable entrepreneurs and celebrities would concur. Meetings go on for much too long and accomplish far too little. I used to agree, but I'm not so sure now. As an executive, you still have work that is solely dependent on you, and getting that work done in a day jam-packed with meetings might feel impossible. However, as an executive, you have direct reports, and there are teams that rely on my assistance. To provide meaningful help, you must first understand what is going on. Not every detail, but enough background and frame to provide significant assistance.It is your responsibility to serve as an effective sounding board and to assist your direct reports in putting their problems into a broader framework. Look, this takes time, especially in one-on-one and small group sessions. If you want to develop mechanisms that support a great corporate culture, you must be accessible, and by available, I mean frequent holy one-on-ones and small team meetings. If you haven't already started holding these meetings, please do so this week. If you are, I have a few suggestions to make them even more helpful. To begin with, keep in mind that one-on-one time is not about you. This is an excellent chance to assist your direct report.This might imply that they talked about their weekend for a while. It may appear to be analysing a recent achievement or defeat. It might be dealing with an HR problem. It might be a casual conversation. Regardless, this is a special moment for them as well. How does this appear? Is there anything you can do or refrain from doing to make it simpler for you to work with me? If one of us is out of town, you should try to reschedule the meeting for the following week. If that's not possible, you move the meeting to the next week, but you seldom meet fewer than three times a month. Surprisingly, sticking to frequent one-on-one sessions has considerably reduced the number of drop-in meetings that have occurred. You have an open door policy, and people are welcome to interrupt you at any time, but frequent one-on-one meetings have naturally encouraged your team to just drop in for emergencies since they know you're accessible to them to think through all of the other things at your weekly one-on-one. You also have a one-hour bi-weekly meeting for your core operating personnel. This meeting, like the one-on-ones, is actually for the team. You spend the first half hour providing brief individual updates and the second half hour attempting to address specific urgent issues through a group discussion. Your CFO just informed you that he believes this will be the most productive meeting we hold.You can get a lot done by catching up with each other, asking smart questions, and solving genuine challenges. All of that effort implies that people feel linked to what they're doing as well as to one another, which promotes morale. So, what are your thoughts on meetings? Have you scheduled the appropriate meetings at the appropriate frequency? Have you made the most of your time? Have you made listening to and supporting your team a priority? Being available is challenging and takes time that you may not believe you have, but consider how much time you'll save by getting more out of the few critical encounters. Create room for being accessible in very consistent ways by establishing these basic procedures, one-on-ones, and small team gatherings.Don't underestimate how pleasant leisure with coworkers may help connection development, trust, and morale when you consider constructing processes to support creating a strong business culture. If you want to build a fantastic business culture, schedule play dates for your employees. With office ping pong and foosball, kombucha or beer on tap, and communal lunches, it appears like the IT sector has perfected the leisure meets work combination. Scheduling play dates resembles this and more. You have a year-end party and a summer BBQ where employees may bring their families, and you've even fielded softball and basketball recreation league teams.Your director of business operations is a fantastic pitcher. These sponsored programmes encourage employees to simply hang out and have fun together. You think that by scheduling time for employees to play together, they will form personal ties within the workplace. As people across lines and between levels come to know each other a little better, these linkages assist in breaking down silos. Now, when you explore these options for your own business, please keep one thing in mind. Make an appearance. Leaders may believe that if they do not attend the celebration, it will go better. Who wants to hang out with their boss, let alone their boss's boss? However, this way of thinking is incorrect.Play dates allow you to be a genuine person, not simply a title. So you must attend the party. Remember that play dates aren't merely for making cross-functional contacts. They also foster links between organizational tiers. They are an essential, deliberate chance for managers and directors to meet frontline personnel and supervisors. That means you'll have the opportunity to work in the room and get to know your teammates. It is vital to cultivate skip-level trust through building these relationships across levels. So set aside some time and go. Run a quick mental assessment to see whether you already have chances like this in your business. Are they assisting you? Are they creating possibilities for cross-functional and cross-layer relationships?If so, keep going and stay involved. If not, what modifications do you need to make? Remember that your ultimate objective is to create a fantastic business culture, and organising play dates is an important part of that.

At your company, you talk a lot about hiring for culture. Yes, every employee has a base level of expertise. But what about cultural fit? It's a major event. You probably spend the majority of your week with coworkers, which is more time than you get to spend with your partner or children. Getting along is a huge thing. You don't have to be best friends, but you do need to build a trusted team that is dedicated to some common aims. While you may discuss mission and culture during the interview, your onboarding process is the first true chance to instil new team members with company values. You've been working to improve our procedure for onboarding volunteers and staff at my organization.After many years of managers trying to onboard their team members in silos, you're moving to a cohort approach that's worked incredibly well for our education programme, bringing on camp workers at the beginning of summer. And for your guest services team, which takes on groups of part-time employees as we scale up for busy seasons. Most firms that are rapidly growing employ a similar cohort method, which I strongly recommend. Even more crucial than attempting to onboard people in cohorts, you must create a culture-centric onboarding approach that involves the heart, head, and hands.Allow me to explain. For starters, people are most interested when they can express themselves emotionally. Engaging the hearts of your new recruits through onboarding appears to be as simple as assisting the cohort in getting to know one another. It entails showing each new recruit how their labour is worthwhile. Perhaps you could share the history of your company. Perhaps you could provide some context or explain your motivation. You'll also need to get into their heads. Onboarding is an excellent moment to outline how work is done in your business.You know that, for better or worse, work is accomplished through collaborative partnerships within your business. And it is critical to help new recruits comprehend this. For you, onboarding is an early chance to establish clear expectations about open communication, collaborative decision-making, and the value of team trust. Finally, onboarding provides an opportunity to solidify each new hire's common knowledge of your business through active experience. You are not a phantom thinker or feeler. Your new recruits aren't either.You provide new workers with on-the-job training and behind-the-scenes experience. You enjoy meals together and spend the majority of your training time engaging new workers in role-playing. These physical exercises assist in cementing the common feeling of being a part of a team. Get people to play games together or work together to solve a real-world problem. Make anything you do dynamic and purposeful. Remember that onboarding is a vital time to engage your newest, most enthusiastic team members in the type of workplace culture that you want to cultivate. Don't pass up this chance.

Summing Up

Without trust, you'll end up with a broken organization with slow-moving teams. A company with a low level of trust is like a jet without gasoline.The cost of a lack of workplace trust or a culture of trust is much higher than you may realize. HR departments at many companies complain that regular interactions aren't happening frequently enough. Creating a strong corporate culture is a continuous effort that is well worth your time. Cultivating a culture of trust is a difficult task for leaders. Good leaders understand that treating everyone equally and respectfully is an important component of building a trusting atmosphere. Give constructive criticism and positive comments frequently so that others understand where you're coming from and what you anticipate. Giving your employees your whole trust and believing in their ability to distinguish a bunch of individuals from a team is a sign of trust. The fear of being blamed can cause anxiety and have a negative impact on employee productivity and happiness. Recognizing employees' accomplishments not only motivates them to strive even more, but it also makes them feel connected. If you want to nourish your culture, try cross-pollinating teams by forming working groups. Learning to listen properly is perhaps the most difficult aspect of managing a book group. When it comes to appreciating individuals, it's critical to look beyond their employment. People see each other more clearly as they get to know one another. When you and your team start treating each other as if everyone is acting with good intentions, you promote inquiry and understanding over blame and judgement. Every day, you must catch your staff doing something positive, and when you do, give straightforward, positive comments. Give clear and timely feedback to your direct reports in order to maintain successful working relationships.A healthy culture is based on clarity and trust, and ground rules foster both. It takes effort to work your way through the ground rules, but it's well worth it. Remember that analyzing without assigning blame does not imply avoiding difficult conversations. No progress will be made until all parties involved understand how to improve for future opportunities.

Conclusions

"Excellence is an art won by training and habituation. We do not act rightly because we have virtue or excellence, but we would rather have those things because we have acted rightly. We are what we repeatedly do. Excellence, then, is not an act but a habit."
-Aristotle

It is advised that both employers and workers understand that in order to create an organizational environment where all people are happier, if an employee feels confident in his or her career prospects, he or she will feel more at ease in his or her workplace. As a result, if you want to know why there are such divisions inside the organization, you need look into all of the aforementioned reasons or causes for such discontent. You may also begin doing all of the measures outlined above to you're your organization a fantastic place to work. To summarize, the roles of leadership and management can function in various ways while still being the same when it comes to the development of a company. Effective techniques for managing businesses into the future include developing and methodically arranging recruiting philosophies, institutional regulations, budgeting procedures, incentives, and decision-making approaches.Leadership would be powerless without leadership's efforts asthe backbone of ideas, and leadership would be worthless if it did not provide a systems-based management framework. Leaders that are ethically sound and willing to sacrifice conveniences for aims and objectives strive for innovation and societal betterment. Leadership and management, like the iceberg and the disciplines, are both autonomous and reliant on one another, especially when attaining goals in a learning company. To conclude this trip, it is critical to recognize that whichever leadership or management style is adopted, it must be related to underlying principles. In essence, the iceberg under the surface is not formed in a single day; it is moulded and nourished throughout the course of one's life by natural and social events, assumptions, and fundamental beliefs. It's vital for leaders to recognize their own icebergs and consider how their beliefs influence their leadership styles and management techniques. In order to be successful in a future society, prospective leaders and managers must first define and develop their own particular leadership style.

Organizational success requires both management and leadership. When a company has great administration but no leadership, the result can be suffocating and bureaucratic. In contrast, if an organization lacks management, the result might be meaningless or misdirected change for the sake of change. Organizations must nurture both competent management and skillful leadership in order to be successful. Organizations perform best when internal and external communication channels are flawless. As a result, effective businesses handle data on a constant basis. Information management is the science of processing information to assist managers in making informed decisions. However, the routes through which this information is transmitted should be secured to preserve the security of the organization's private information, which may otherwise be exposed to unwanted third-party intrusion. Culture defines all elements of a firm, including internal and external interactions, in the information system implementation planning strategy. It's crucial to strike a balance between the intended and undesirable effects while encoding and decoding data. As a result, while analysing performance based on feedback, it's critical to treat the voluntarily information with caution in order to foster trust and secrecy, which are at the pinnacle of organizational behaviour.

As a result, as a cure for inclusion and active involvement, which translates into ideal performance, it is vital to balance feedback with the aims of such an organization. In general, risk is seen as a negative aspect in the implementation of new technology in an organization because of the potential for unrealized advantages, technical performance deficiencies, schedule slippage, cost overruns, and worker disengagement. It's critical to have a robust plan in place to handle the risks that come with adopting new concepts like technological efficiency.

There should be systems in place to maintain employees in a healthy and stable state of mind while doing their duties of serving the organization's interests through regulated ethical communication models. Expected behaviour, procedural patterns, and responses to deviations are all defined by these models. The idea underpinning risk estimating and evaluation is that logical inferences may be drawn about the chance of a risk occurring and its possible repercussions.

Setting a goal and then devising a strategy to attain it is a typical practise in any organization. All companies obey the rules, but only a few are able to meet or surpass their goals. The disparity in results is attributable to the organization's strategy. Organizations that can effectively and efficiently execute and manage their resources stand out from the crowd. Motivation, empowerment, and training are the key positive influences on successful organizational behaviour. In order to create a proactive mindset among employees, these elements should be incorporated into a company. Incentives, promotions, awards, and recognition are just a few of the motivation-boosting techniques. The planning component is critical in de-mystifying poor performance as a result of personnel redundancy. Because the degree of success is dependent on social interaction abilities, the appropriate implementation of a competence evaluation system is directly proportionate to employee performance. An emotion testing programme is implemented to assess employees' emotional attitudes toward one another, followed by a counselling session to ensure that employees are concerned about their coworkers' social needs. Because difficulties that each individual experiences on an interpersonal level eventually influence the group, it is critical to build a healthy work environment and personal growth views that apply to all situations in order to enhance productive behaviour. Organizational psychologists should conduct in-depth investigations into each employee's personal life in order to identify which behavioural treatment best matches the individual. A good working environment should be flexible, relevant, and pleasant, all while adhering to measurement criteria that support the intrinsic and extrinsic effects that the environment has on employee performance.

On the other hand, should be tailored to a unique work environment, employee talents, and organizational objectives. Furthermore, the size of an organization and the nature of its responsibilities must be considered. Within each business, numerous elements such as incentives, advancement, and a structured feedback system impact organizational behaviour. Policies geared towards balancing performance and conduct, on the other hand, should be connected with an organization's goals in order to be effective.

Every leader has a distinct perspective about what makes a company culture successful. However, healthy workplaces share certain similarities, such as worker autonomy, open communication, clear direction, genuine relationships, and aligned values. Creating, scaling, and maintaining an authentic company culture is an ongoing and intentional process. As the business landscape and global climate changes, corporate culture needs to grow to fit worker needs and desires. Reading organizational culture books helps professionals gain the skills and mindsets necessary to make their companies great places to work. The effort to support employees ultimately pays off, as companies with great work cultures see reduced turnover, inspire more brand loyalty, and are better equipped to weather inevitable adversity.

Suggestions

"The excellence and inspiration of truth is in the pursuit, not in the mere having of it. The pursuit of all truth is a kind of gymnastics; a man swings from one truth with higher strength to gain another. The continual glory is the possibility opening before us." -Edwin Hubbel Chapin

A workplace should be a location where a person may be inspired to contribute their talents and abilities to the company's overall development as well as their own professional development. It is a place where an employee and an employer collaborate to improve their professional pleasure. It's possible that a person working in a hostile workplace will have difficulty fulfilling his or her obligations and responsibilities. According to the author, "a happy employee is more likely to be innovative and productive." Furthermore, happy employees are a valuable asset to any company. As a result, it is critical for businesses to make their staff happy.

Organizational productivity is influenced by the work environment. Building a better place to work is closely tied to having a pleasant work environment. Employees are more likely to perform effectively in a better environment, which aids the company's success. The key question is, "What makes an organization a wonderful place to work?" and it is likely to be a very subjective one. A variety of elements influence whether an individual finds a place "excellent" or not, including monetary pay, senior appreciation, infrastructure, interesting professional prospects, appropriate career growth, awards and recognition, as well as team support. It is critical to comprehend what makes your organization a fantastic place to work and how to improve it. The following are some of the factors that contribute to or assist in establishing a pleasant working environment for both employees and employers.

- It's important to have a clear vision and goal.

- Critical Communication that works.
- Employees are allowed to grow in a "flexible" manner.
- It encourages meritocracy.
- Having a culture of collaboration.
- Leadership advice that is easily accessible.
- Stay away from politics.
- Employees‘ candid feedback is sought.
- Leadership that is both honest and impartial.
- A more favourable working environment.
- Employees who are passionate and devoted.
- Encourage openness and transparency.
- It also assists in the development of management skills.
- Providing incentives and expressing gratitude.
- Keep only what you require in your immediate vicinity.
- Maintain a clean work environment in order to avoid neck and back pain.
- Keeping plants, air fresheners, open windows.
- Keep a supply of water and snacks on hand.
- Natural Light and Open Windows for proper brightness and lighting.
- Small victories are celebrated.
- Maintain a comfortable office temperature.
- The hours of employment are flexible.
- Options for working from home.
- Time off is paid indefinitely.
- Financials that are open and transparent.
- Promotions that are not prejudiced.
- Equal acclaim and rewards.
- Tasks are distributed evenly.
- Feedback that is both frequent and open.
- Performance evaluations are both positive and negative.
- Encourage employees to do work that they enjoy, since this will help them advance professionally.

You've been given a list of distinctive characteristics that distinguish a firm as a great place to work so you can see them throughout your job hunt. It is critical to make an employer feel good about his or her working environment, and in order to do so, an employer must begin encouraging employees in his or her office to perform more effectively. As a result, it is critical to motivate firm personnel with some type of professional encouragement, such as promotions or performance recognition. All of these factors contribute to an employee's feeling good or fantastic about their job. A company is a place where all employees and their bosses collaborate and responsibly carry out their responsibilities. It's feasible that this task delivery will profit if they strive to learn from one another.

There may have been instances where an employer acted maturely in handling a critical circumstance, and these experiences may all assist an employee learn from his or her employer in the future. Working in a positive atmosphere may necessitate some degree of optimism among employees and employers, but the fact is that this may be achieved by encouraging healthy competition among these companies and their employees to do better in their jobs. These contests may be introduced in order to establish a realistic aim for the financial year-end competition. This type of competition is frequently performed in the marketing or sales departments to motivate employees. There is a frequent type of error that most employees make when working in the workplace. For example, an employee exclusively talks with his or her coworkers in his or her department and never seeks contact with anybody else in the department. This type of behaviour might severely limit the options available to the employee. As a result, if an employee tries to mix or communicate with other office staff members, there is a chance that the employee may wind up with a large number of coworkers. Some companies provide entertaining acts or events in the office on special occasions. For a successful completion, it is also recommended that all of the company's workers participate in such activities, either as participants or as volunteers. As a result, all of these efforts may help to create a climate that allows all of the company's employees to feel more at ease in their workplace. If an employer or employee wants to feel good about their job, there is a simple thing they can do to maintain a healthy working relationship. It's possible that a junior employer starts denigrating a senior employee for no apparent reason, and this creates a negative environment for both corporate employees. As a result, in order to avoid such conflict between workers, an employer must speak with them in order to address issues and establish a positive work environment for their own good. It is normal in any firm for most workers or employers to demand some type of performance appreciation from their superiors in order to improve their department's performance. As a result, in order to meet such goals in the workplace, higher-ups must consider staff performance evaluations in order to motivate and improve their department's performance. To make a firm a place where all of the workers enjoy working together, an employer must create an image that allows other employees to express gratitude for the assistance they have received in the workplace.

Most workers may not be involved in each other's work at times, but when a critical moment occurs in the department, they must help one another, and this support should be recognised as part of the company's goodwill. While strong rivalry among employees may foster a healthy spirit among all employees, certain employees may attempt to share their political expertise in the workplace. Some workers play politics between the employer and the employee in order to create some sort of misunderstanding between them, with the employee eventually benefiting from the corporate politics. Such office politics may wreak havoc on a pleasant working atmosphere. Employees in most companies face some form of communication gap with their bosses as a result of their position or attitude. As a result, that might be a probable cause of the company's imbalance, in which all employees are negative about their workplace. And, in order to avoid such negativity, an employer must remember that all of the company's employees are equal in terms of service delivery. Each firm employee has their own career goals, which may range from person to person.Some employees have higher expectations for their careers, and they work extra hard in their departments to achieve them. As a result, this type of hard work or analysis of superior job ability may help an employee plan his or her future growth in the organization.And this might result in an external force that appears to be beneficial to their career. Many businesses do not value diversity in their workplaces or departments.It's also likely that the majority of their coworkers disagree with their authority as women. When employers learn their higher authority bearer is a woman or a lady, they may ask candidates about their point of view during interviews. This type of gender discrimination might contribute to a negative atmosphere in the workplace.

A firm where all workers work their jobs for the company's overall development must realise one thing: they are a professional family, and they must support each other with whatever problems they experience in their departments. That may happen when a corporation begins to celebrate each employee's accomplishments in order to make them feel like a family. This type of improvement has the potential to improve official settings. Not just the office atmosphere, but every employee must put in some effort to make their workplace a better place for everyone. It is not uncommon for some workers to neglect to execute their jobs and attempt to cause issues for others. This type of employee conduct breeds negativity in them, which might exacerbate the situation at work, leading to him or her being dismissed from his or her position. Most organizations want their workers or employers to back them up in their organizational decisions. And it is common for some employees or employers to disagree with the company's choice. Instead of responding irrationally, those employees might consider making a decision that will benefit each of them in the long run. Instead of behaving irrationally, those workers may think about making a decision that will help each of them in their greatest career, and while there may be some troubles along the way, it will eventually be over. A successful company must recognize that innovative product ideas may be the key to its success. These novel concepts have the potential to transform the commercial market. Eventually, all of the company's workers begin to feel safe in their assigned departmental responsibilities. As a result, a corporation should be open to new ideas for the company's and its employees' overall development. Working in a firm may appear to be a difficult task at first, but if an employee attempts to grasp his or her responsibilities, it will no longer be so difficult. For several reasons, the working atmosphere in the office might change from day to day. To avoid this, all personnel must be honest and disciplined in their assigned duties.

Pick a stress reliever that a company offers: To relieve stress from office work and responsibilities, a company might organise a stress reliever activity for its employees, and some firms do so to help their employees feel more at ease in the workplace. It's possible that the majority of companies that utilise such stress relievers have the highest rate of excellent workers in their offices. As a result, it is critical to comprehend the importance of such stress-relieving activities. In every business, time management is critical. And this should be strictly followed in all businesses.It is vital to have such time-management skills in the workplace. Some organizations follow rigorous restrictions in the name of time management, and they put their employees on such a tight schedule that they wind up dealing with unfavourable conditions at work.

For the sake of the firm's wellbeing, a corporation must implement a fair time management method to minimise such strain. An employee who is new to his or her workplace and worried about his or her responsibilities, for example, may be uneasy being around such highly competent colleagues. At that point, he or she must make an impression as a nice person, which can only be accomplished by his or her ability to impress all members of the workforce. This first impression of his or her personality might either help or hurt him or her at work.

Managing a positive work environment is essential for maximising employee productivity. Do you look forward to another amazing day at work when you wake up every morning, or do they drag yourselves to work every day? Working people nowadays spend about a third of their lives at work, with a significant portion of their productive lives committed to their companies. Now, you've developed a strong value system in which we aim to establish a trusting connection with our employees in order to make the company seem more like a family. The primary components on which you build your human resource techniques are dialogue, feedback, communication, and trust, and these values constitute the core of our high-performance culture. Each employee is a precious human resource who must be nourished, cultivated, and valued. Human resources, unlike stocks, money, and other inanimate resources, are not replaceable. Individual training requires time and effort, and changing people at whim is neither easy nor in the best interests of the organization. As a result, each organization's primary value should be respect for its people. If you treat your employees with dignity and respect as a manager, they will immediately reciprocate to the organization. Respect your subordinates, communicate with them, listen to their ideas, implement their suggestions, and make them feel appreciated. This method not only helps employees feel appreciated, but it also provides us with a release valve for any pent-up tension or feelings. The pattern and means of working in an organization change as the times change.

Because mobile phones make communication so easy, employees are now expected to be available 24 hours a day, seven days a week, whether it's Saturday or Sunday. This kind of adaptability should not only be expected of students, but also encouraged. As a result, stringent log-in times may be replaced with flexi hours, and employees can be granted a few days of work from home to offer them a more comfortable and accommodating atmosphere. This is critical in order to retain competent and experienced personnel, particularly women, who may want more professional flexibility in order to balance the demands of parenting. Furthermore, according to a recent poll on workplace flexibility conducted by HR service provider Randstad, up to 53% of Indian respondents favour telecommuting. As a manager, you must ensure that an employee's contributions to your organization are never overlooked. Praise should be freely given in your organization; this motivates employees and makes them feel valued. While performance gaps and mismanagement must be identified and remedied, managers should prioritise delivering solutions rather than simply blaming individuals. Even after putting their all into a project, a team may not be able to achieve the anticipated outcomes. As a manager, your strategy should be to review each completed project for flaws and errors, and then teach your employees improved execution techniques.

Young and inexperienced leaders, in particular, are continuously in need of direction and mentorship from more experienced executives. Is your company a monolith when it comes to people, or does it have a varied workforce in terms of gender, linguistics, racial, ethnic, and religious backgrounds? Experience reveals that diverse organizations with a diversified workforce (gender, linguistic, racial, ethnic, and religious) are more open to new ideas because they are exposed to a wider range of viewpoints and have a more flexible cognitive process. It will always be a rewarding place to work at an organization where employees support and aid one another at all times rather than engage in cutthroat rivalry. Employees who are always competing with one another foster office politics and degrade the workplace atmosphere. Being a part of social activities gives workers, especially the younger ones, a sense of increased purpose and usefulness. Involving workers in the firm's beneficial social activities gives them another reason to stay with the company.

Working for a good employer is enjoyable, gratifying, and challenging. While job hunting, look for organizations with happy employees, attractive perks, and a healthy corporate culture. These are all indicators of a fantastic place to work. According to a Nielsen study on corporate social responsibility conducted in 2014, as many as 67 percent of those polled chose to work for socially responsible businesses. It's critical to have personnel that are educated to support each other rather than pull the rug out from under each other.

A great place to work values and supports its workers while also pushing them to advance within the organization. Managers and workers at these organizations have a mutual trust and regard for one another, as well as a shared dedication to individual and corporate success. Great organizations make an effort to address the financial, mental, physical, and emotional requirements of their employees. Employees are more productive, pleased, and eager to stay at the firm for the long haul as a consequence.

The common beliefs, attitudes, and behaviours of a corporation and its employees are referred to as company culture. Honesty, self-improvement, and communication may be among a company's basic principles. A company's culture is influenced by a variety of factors, including communication, style of management, benefits, traditions, transparency. You may be more involved, contented, and productive if you work for a firm that has a great corporate culture or values and attitudes that you share. Managers trust their employees to work hard and make excellent decisions in healthy work environments. Employees trust company leaders to assist and encourage them, and coworkers trust each other to strive toward common goals. A reliable group is driven to work hard and is involved in and happy with their task. Employees in a fair workplace believe they are compensated fairly and have the same opportunities as their coworkers. In a firm that values justice, employees are also less likely to face politics, bias, and favouritism. If an organization treats everyone equally and fairly, employees are more inclined to operate as a team. Open communication fosters workplace trust and avoids misunderstandings. The following are signs of successful and transparent communication. Look for a company that values open lines of communication and takes employee feedback into account when making decisions. Working for a company that is continually developing new products, strategies, and procedures may be a thrilling experience. Employees in innovative organizations are encouraged to take chances, exchange ideas, and provide suggestions. As a consequence, employees are more motivated and proud of their job as a consequence, and the firm has more opportunities to expand and flourish as a result. Look for a firm that is a market leader and where employees feel comfortable discussing their thoughts with management. Employees that are invested and interested in the outcome of their job are commonly found in great firms. They are committed to the company's objective and strive toward common goals that go beyond sales and earnings. Furthermore, the firm's leadership is interested in and engaged in the day-to-day operations of the company, and they are attentive to queries and suggestions.

Working for an organization is likely to be a terrific place to work if it is a dream job for the majority of individuals in your sector. Look for organizations with strong brands and competitive pricing. Check to see whether a company has received any awards for the best workplace in your sector or region. Talented employees are drawn to great firms, and they often remain for a long time. Employees' trust and dedication to addressing problems and accomplishing goals may be earned by companies that are upfront about their challenges, accomplishments, and everyday operations. Meetings or briefings on the company's issues and triumphs on a regular basis. Open-book management refers to a management style in which the company's executives disclose financial and other key information to all employees. When confronted with financial, operational, or strategic issues, leaders who solicit employee comments or suggestions are more likely to succeed.

Everyone's viewpoint matters in a transparent workplace, and everyone shares in the company's success. Employees like to work with leaders that are confident, effective, and fair. Good leadership not only keeps people engaged, motivated, and goal-oriented, but it also helps firms prosper financially. Managers that treat their staff like adults encourage them to make decisions and work on their own. They also value their staff, solicit feedback, and reward them for their hard work and good contributions.

Great places to work have employees with different levels of expertise, backgrounds, and beliefs. They recognise the importance of having a diverse staff and make an effort to employ a diverse group of people. A diverse workforce is more likely to generate intriguing ideas and innovative solutions. A diverse workplace is also friendly to new employees and encourages morale among existing ones.

About The Author

Dr. Amit is the founder of Accumentor India, a consultancy firm set up by him in the human resource solution space, which is focused on developing processes for people. It offers consultancy in learning management, mentorship, performance coaching, training and development, psychometric analysis, HR processes and interventions. He was formerly the Director of Expertell Learning Point.

Dr. Amit Das is an experienced sales, training, and learning professional with more than 20 years of working history in the healthcare, medical devices, and learning management industries. Dr. Amit is a seasoned training professional with rich experience and a successful track record in aligning learning and training solutions to key business strategy with a strong focus on flawless execution excellence to facilitate individual, business divisional, and organisational performance. He keeps relentless focus on measuring training impact and ROI, people capability building graphs, training process governance, performance coaching, and strategic thinking. These have been some of his key individual success traits. His core capabilities include performance coaching, designing training and development frameworks and facilitation of technical skill building, psychometric assessment and analysis, competency framework development and assessments, content design and facilitation of soft skills and leadership programmes, E-Learning Platform development, Learning Management Systems, Learning Impact Measurement, Talent Analysis and Performance Management System Review, Performance Coaching and Counselling.

His interests are in the areas of leadership development, coaching competency, mentorship, and motivational complexities related to organisational issues. His hobbies include public speaking, content creation, and reading books.

He has a Ph.D. and a Fellowship in strategic learning, along with his first class degrees in Human Resource Management and Corporate Laws from the top business schools in India. He is a certified professional coach from U.K. and behavioral coach from U.S.A.

References

- *Managing Transitions: Making the Most of Change by William Bridges and Susan Bridges*
- *Our Iceberg Is Melting: Changing and Succeeding Under Any Conditions by John Kotter and Holger Rathgeber*
- *Change (the) Management: Why We as Leaders Must Change for the Change to Last by Al Comeaux*
- *Doing Agile Right: Transformation Without Chaos by Darrell Rigby, Sarah Elk and Steve Berez*
- *You're It: Crisis, Change, and How to Lead When It Matters Most by Leonard J. Marcus, Eric J. McNulty, et al.*
- *Reinventing Organizations: A Guide to Creating Organizations Inspired by the Next Stage in Human Consciousness by by Frederic Laloux*
- *Work Rules! (Insights from Inside Google That Will Transform How You Live and Lead) by Laszlo Bock*
- *Delivering Happiness: A Path to Profits, Passion, and Purpose by Tony Hsieh*
- *The Culture Code: The Secrets of Highly Successful Groups by Daniel Coyl*
- *No Rules Rules: Netflix and the Culture of Reinvention by Reed Hastings and Erin Meye*
- *Powerful: Building a Culture of Freedom and Responsibility by Patty McCord*
- *The Culture Blueprint: A Guide to Building the High-Performance Workplace by Robert Richman*
- *The Best Place to Work: The Art and Science of Creating an Extraordinary Workplace by Ron Friedman*
- *Humanocracy: Creating Organizations as Amazing as the People Inside Them by by Gary Hamel and Michele Zanini*
- *Fusion: How Integrating Brand and Culture Powers the World's Greatest Companies by Denise Lee Yohn*

- *The Culture Book: When Culture Clicks (How to Build Incredible Culture from 32 Companies Who Have Done It) by Weeva and Culturati, Patty McCord, et al*
- *Courageous Cultures: How to Build Teams of Micro-Innovators, Problem Solvers, and Customer Advocates by by Karin Hurt and David Dye*
- *The Culture Quotient: Ten Dimensions of a High-Performance Culture by Greg Besner*
- *The Insider's Guide to Culture Change: Creating a Workplace That Delivers, Grows, and Adapts by Siobhan McHale*
- *Radical Candor by Kim Malone Scott*
- ***Becoming the Best: Build a World-Class Organization Through Values-Based Leadership by Harry M. Kraemer, 2015***
- *Musa, P. and Tulay, G., Investigating the impact of organizational excellence and leadership on achieving business performance: An exploratory study of Turkish firms, SAM Advance Management Journal*
- *Shirvani, A. and Iranban, S., Organizational excellence performance and human force productivity promotion: A case study of South Zagros Oil and Gas production company, Iran, European Online Journal of Natural and Social Sciences*
- *Zgodavova, K., Hudec, O, and Palfy, P., Culture and Quality: Insight into foreign organizations in Slovakia, Total Quality Management & Business Excellence*
- *Peters, T.J. and Waterman, R. H., In search of Excellence: Lessons from America's Best Run Companies, (First Edition), Harper & Row, New York, USA*
- *Harrington, H.J., The Five Pillars of Organizational Excellence, paper presented at 9th International Convention on Quality Improvement*
- *Methurst, D. and Richards, D., The Fundamental Concepts of Organizational Excellence: A Blueprint of Success, D & D*

Printed by Libri Plureos GmbH in Hamburg,
Germany